Matter

Maynooth Studies in Local History

SERIES EDITOR Raymond Gillespie

This volume is one of six short books published in the Maynooth Studies in Local History series in 2011. Like their predecessors they range widely, both chronologically and geographically, over the local experience in the Irish past. That local experience is presented in the complex and contested social worlds of which it is part. As such they reflect the divide between popular beliefs about women healers in Kildare and the music and dancing in a great house in the same county, the military confrontations of revolutionary Galway and the legal confrontations of breach of promise cases in Limerick and the differing tenant experience of eviction and re-colonisation on the earl of Clanricarde's lands in 19th-century Galway and the colonization of Ráth Cairn with Irish speakers in the 20th century. These local experiences cannot be a simple chronicling of events relating to an area within administrative or geographically determined boundaries since understanding a local world presents much more complex challenges for the historian. It is a reconstruction of the socially diverse worlds of the poor as well as the rich and a consideration of those who took widely contrasting positions on the political issues that preoccupied local communities in Ireland. Reconstructing such diverse local worlds relies on understanding what the people of the different communities that made up the localities of Ireland had in common and what drove them apart. Understanding the assumptions, often unspoken, around which these local societies operated is the key to recreating the world of the Irish past and reconstructing the way in which those who inhabited those worlds lived their daily lives. In addressing these issues, studies such as those presented in these short books, together with their predecessors, are at the forefront of Irish historical research and represent some of the most innovative and exciting work being undertaken in Irish history today. They also provide models which others can follow up and adapt in their own studies of the Irish past. In such ways will we understand better the regional diversity of Ireland and the social and cultural basis for that diversity. If they also convey something of the vibrancy and excitement of the world of Irish local history today they will have achieved at least some of their purpose.

Maynooth Studies in Local History: Number 96

Matters of deceit

Breach of promise to marry cases in nineteenth- and twentieth-century Limerick

Maria Luddy

FOUR COURTS PRESS

Set in 10pt on 12pt Bembo by
Carrigboy Typesetting Services for
FOUR COURTS PRESS LTD
7 Malpas Street, Dublin 8, Ireland
www.fourcourtspress.ie
and in North America for
FOUR COURTS PRESS
c/o ISBS, 920 N.E. 58th Avenue, Suite 300, Portland, OR 97213.

ISBN 978–1–84682–294–0

Printed in England
by Antony Rowe Ltd, Chippenham, Wilts.

Contents

Acknowledgments

I am grateful to the Arts and Humanities Research Council (AHRC) for their funding of the History of Marriage in Ireland, 1660–1925 project, co-directed with Professor Mary O'Dowd of Queen's University, Belfast. The information in this book derives from that project. I would like to thank Dr Katie Barclay and Dr John Bergin for their invaluable research work. I am grateful to Dr Frank Eissa Barroso for his efforts in collating all of the breach of promise material. I want to thank Professor Raymond Gillespie for his patience in waiting for a manuscript that was always 'almost done'. I am going to surprise Hazel Campbell by mentioning her and thanking her for all the 'other work'. As ever, Virginia Crossman has read all of this, again and again.

1. Introduction

In Co. Limerick in 1870 Sarah Sheehan, aged about 23 years and the daughter of a deceased farmer who left her a fortune of £200, sued Thomas Stack, a widower, of about 40, for breach of promise to marry. The couple was deemed to be of the same social rank and Stack held a 'well-stocked farm in county Kerry'. The couple had first met in February 1869, and it was friends of the defendant who proposed the marriage. Consultations were held between both parties, an interview took place at Sheehan's brother's house and the marriage was arranged. The dowry or 'fortune' to be brought by Sheehan was £150 to be paid at the time of the marriage and a further £50 after twelve months. Stack, it was noted, was untrustworthy and 'seemed to have regularly fallen in love at first sight'. Sheehan had made arrangements for the marriage ceremony and purchased a wedding dress. Stack sent his brother-in-law to tell Sheehan that his friends disapproved of the marriage, and claimed he needed the permission, which was not forthcoming, of the aged maiden aunt with whom he lived. The jury took the side of the plaintiff and awarded her £200 in damages.[1] This was one of the hundreds of cases taken by women against men who had reneged on their promise to marry. And this was a relatively clear-cut case, the marriage settlement had been agreed, Sarah had done all of the necessary preparation by organizing the ceremony and buying the wedding outfit, and Stack had shown himself to be unreliable and dishonourable. The substantial damages awarded recognized that Sarah had been unjustly treated by Stack. Her reputation was publicly vindicated by the court case and the award of damages.

There were many routes to marriage in 19th- and 20th-century Ireland. Women were abducted, couples fell in love, families arranged marriages, where couples did not accept arrangements they ran away or eloped together. Couples lived together without getting married, there were bigamists, and those who broke promises to marry. Marriage was of significance to women and men for social, emotional and economic reasons. Society considered women's natural place to be in the home, tending to the needs of husband and children. Married women had greater status than unmarried women. The most acceptable way to form families was through marriage and, as in all time periods, both men and women desired children. Economic stability, though not necessarily guaranteed by marriage, was an inducement to marriage for many women, especially in a society where paid employment opportunities for them were limited. Women did of course work, but many engaged in unpaid work on family farms, and in family businesses, as daughters or wives. The most common paid occupation for employed women was domestic service, and in 1891 about 255,000 women worked as servants while another 139,000 unmarried women did similar, though unpaid work, for parents or brothers. By 1911 one working woman in three was, according to the census, in service. This was considered a respectable form of employment and was believed to offer good training for when a woman married and created her own household. Women also worked in industrial employments in cities such as Belfast, and to a lesser extent, in Dublin. By the end of the 19th century professional employment as trained nurses and clerks, and occupations within medicine and the law were opening to women. Despite the opening of new fields of employment for women there was a contraction in the labour market by the end of the 19th century. In 1901, 430,000 women in Ireland were employed; 20 years earlier the figure was 641,000.[2] The lack of employment opportunities for women in Ireland contributed to a high rate of female emigration. Women formed about 48 per cent of all emigrants between 1850 and 1890, and 50 per cent from 1890 to 1920. Between 1885 and 1920 almost 700,000, mostly unmarried women, left Ireland.[3]

In 1807 one commentator observed that in Ireland 'an unmarried man … or a woman … is rarely to be met in the country parts.'[4] Before the Famine only a small proportion of the population did not marry, 8–12 per cent of men over 55 and 12–15 per cent of women over 55.[5] The proportion of 45–54 year-old men who had never married rose from 12 per cent in 1851 to 27 per cent in 1911; among women in the same age group the rise was from 13 to 25 per cent.[6] In the post-Famine period the need for a man to earn a reasonable wage or to be in possession of a farm before he could marry would have inhibited his marital opportunities, just as the lack of a dowry or 'fortune' would have impeded women's opportunity to marry. The usual pattern for strong farmers, both in pre-and post-Famine Ireland, was to consolidate their land holdings. This in turn supported individual inheritance, where the farm was left often, but not always, to the eldest son; sometimes a middle or younger son could inherit. Less frequently a daughter might inherit, though in that case it was often dependent on some suitable man marrying into the farm. Parents decided when to give up the farm and sometimes the wait to inherit could be a long one. Late marriage patterns in farming families may be explained to some extent by the hold that fathers, and widows, had on a farm, unwilling to relinquish that control for a considerable time. In 1871, 43 per cent of all women aged 15–45 were married. In 1911 only 36 per cent of women in this age range were married. By 1911 the average age of marriage for women was 29 while that of men was 33 years. Jurors would have been aware of the obstacles facing those wishing to marry in the period, especially in post-Famine Ireland. They would have recognized the importance of a woman's reputation to her marital prospects, and the need for a dowry, no matter how small. Whether women who were 'jilted' went on to marry is unclear from the available evidence, though a considerable number of the men, most often the defendants in these cases, did marry.

In 1841 in Limerick county, the focus of this study, 38,203 men and 39,342 women between the ages of 17 and 56 and over were married, about 49 per cent of the population in that age range. In Limerick city in the same year 7,226 men and 8,013 women in the same age groups were married, accounting for about 51 per cent of the population. In 1881, in the age group between 15 and 100, 24,004 men and 24,409 women were married. This accounted for about 42 per cent of the population of the county. At the same time 7,265 men within the county between the ages of 15 and 40 were unmarried, while 22,870 women in the same age group remained single. In Co. Limerick in 1911, 18,769 men and 19,027 women in the age group between 15 and 100 were married, about 37 per cent of the county's population above 15 years of age, while 29,114 men and 24,435 in the same age group remained single. As with the trend in Ireland generally, marriage rates in the period from 1841 to 1911 were declining in the county. Opportunities for marriage for men appear to have been greater than those for women of the same age groups.[7]

A breach of promise to marry is a fundamental break of a promise, by either a man or woman, to carry through a marriage. Usually an engagement period precedes a marriage and the couple make promises to marry sometime in the future. In common law such promise was a legally binding contract, and if broken the responsible party could be sued for a breach of promise to marry. However, breach of promise cases were not always straightforward; the law recognized that such promises were often personal in nature and difficulties might arise to prevent or make the proposed marriage untenable. Such promises were like a contract and like other contracts some sort of evidence was required if a prosecution was to be successful and damages awarded.[8] In Ireland almost all the breach of promise cases, from the late 18th to the early 20th centuries, were brought by women.[9] Essentially, the woman who brought the case was seeking money, 'damages', for a broken promise of marriage. In taking a case she was implying that her reputation had suffered, that her ability to find a suitable husband to support her was perhaps irreparably impaired, and that her future was bleak and she was condemned to spinsterhood.

It was primarily through the courts that breach of promise to marry cases came to public light, providing lawyers with lucrative incomes and newspapers with titillating stories for their reading audience. The actual court cases themselves were a form of public entertainment and the court room the arena of performance for witnesses, barristers, judges, and, after 1869, defendants and plaintiffs. Exploring the history of breach of promise cases in Ireland allows an insight into courtship rituals, reveals the significance of monetary considerations in marriage settlements and the value that was placed on women's (and men's) reputations. Such history also alerts us to the importance of family in either protecting their children from unsuitable marriage partners, or pursuing appropriate ones. Issues of class are highlighted in some cases and reveal the unwillingness of society, at least as expressed by jurors, to condone cross-class alliances. Furthermore, exploring breach of promise cases suggests ways of understanding ideas of romance and love in Irish courtship. While it is evident that Irish marriages were expected, at least by the end of the 19th century, to include some level of affection they were primarily enterprises that were shaped by social and economic compatibility. While impossible to quantify, one of the facts to emerge from a study of breach of promise cases is the prevalence of premarital sex. Jurors do not appear to punish women where evidence of premarital sexual activity, often signified by the birth of an illegitimate child, comes to light. It is possible to argue that there was a greater tolerance of such activity within society than we have hitherto been led to believe. The prominence of breach of promise cases in the newspapers throughout the period also suggests that rather than being hidden, issues relating to sexuality, and how people conducted their love lives, found very public expression through these reports. The range of news coverage on divorce, breach of promise, adultery and seduction cases, not to mention items on sexual assault which appear to have been less widely covered, suggests that the press, both local and national, was a significant medium of sexual gossip for the reading public.

It is my intention in this short book to look at a number of specific breach of promise to marry cases for Co. Limerick from the 19th to the 20th centuries. Despite one barrister, noting in jest in 1873, that Abbeyfeale, Co. Limerick, was 'notorious for breach of promise cases',[10] focusing on Limerick offers a useful way to assess and interrogate breach of promise cases more generally in Ireland. A good range of cases, both rural and urban, are available for the county, and there is a considerable variety in the class backgrounds of plaintiffs and defendants. Much of what can be said about cases relating to Limerick holds true for cases in the rest of Ireland and here I will juxtapose similar cases to explore how a local history can both illuminate and reflect what is going on more generally in the county in relation to a specific subject. Before examining any cases in detail it will be useful to discuss the sources for these cases and the numbers of cases taken more generally over the period. It is not possible to provide an accurate breakdown of the number of cases that were specific to a particular county. Often cases were heard in the Dublin or Cork courts, and the place of residence or origin of either the plaintiff or defendant was not provided. Sometimes cases heard in Limerick related to couples who resided in Counties Clare or Tipperary. At times the reports are so short that the only reference to place provided refers to the court in which the case was heard.

Before 1865 it is difficult to gather accurate figures about the numbers of breach of promise cases that were pursued through the Irish courts. I have collected information, for the period from 1760 to 1919, on 514 cases that went to court. After 1865, when statistics of cases were reported annually in the Judicial and Criminal Statistics for Ireland, 401 cases went to court.[11] Between 1764 and 1864, 138 cases have been recorded. This figure is very likely to be underestimated as before 1865 no official figures were kept. Breach of promise cases were taken overwhelmingly by women and unless specifically noted plaintiffs in this text refer to women and defendants refer to men. Of the 138 cases identified and tried between 1764 and 1864 for example, only 14 of the plaintiffs were men; after 1865 there were at least 12 male plaintiffs. Information on all of the cases comes from the newspapers, primarily the *Freeman's Journal*, the *Belfast Newsletter*, and the *Irish Times*. A number of local papers were also sampled including the *Connaught Journal*, the *Ballina Impartial*, and *Finn's Leinster Journal*. Sometimes the reports are a few lines, but many take up whole columns that can run on for days. The reports from these papers cover most of the country and the more local papers also copied the reports appearing in the national press. Clearly the data does not include every breach of promise case but I believe it provides us with enough information to make some legitimate observations about these kinds of cases.

A number of Irish women appear to have taken cases in the English courts. For instance, it was reported in 1869 that a 'Miss Morony, a young Irish lady of great personal attraction and of good position in the county Clare', obtained £2,000 damages in an action against an officer of the army in Croydon assizes.[12] Similarly, in 1873 Miss Kate Humphrey, the daughter of a Dublin solicitor, sued Nicholas Vincent Wise, a medical student and a gentleman farmer near Cork, in the Court of Common Pleas in London.[13] In Victorian England it was believed that breach of promise to marry cases had become 'epidemic' by the 1860s. Ginger Frost claims that in the decades between the 1860s and 1890s the numbers of such trials nearly doubled, with an average of 34 cases a year being brought in the 1860s rising to an average of 67 cases a year by the 1890s.[14] In Ireland in the decade of the 1860s about 69 cases went to trial and this had decreased only slightly in the 1890s when a total of 62 cases were brought to court. The level of breach of promise cases in Ireland did rise in the first decade of the 20th century when between 1900 and 1909, 87 cases came before the courts. There was a steady flow of such cases appearing in the Irish courts throughout the period, though the numbers never reached 'epidemic' proportions.

Given the type of case breach of promise is, it is also unlikely that every case came to court and indeed matters may have been settled out of court to prevent embarrassment to either party. Frost has noted in her work on breach of promise cases in England between 1859 and 1921 at least a fifth of the cases were withdrawn before they got to the actual courtroom.[15] In Ireland, for the period under review, at least 110 cases were entered for court proceedings but were either withdrawn or settled out of court. In 1857, for instance, the case between Devereux and Henry, settled for £300, was cancelled just as it came to court.[16] A small number of breach of promise cases were considered 'notorious' and were reprinted as pamphlets. These can offer deeper insights and more detail than provided in the press reports but only a handful of such cases have been found.

The public maintained an overwhelming curiosity in these cases throughout the period. The accounts of breach of promise cases were a regular feature of the national and local press, and papers such as the *Belfast Newsletter*, the *Freeman's Journal* and the *Irish Times* reported cases that came before the English courts. Indeed, about a quarter of the reports appearing in the Irish press on breach of promise cases were cases from the English courts. In 1890 the *Freeman's Journal* noted that 'actions for breach of promise have not been of late years very frequent. Such of them as could be considered large and important suits have been few indeed.' However, the same paper then reported on a London 'May to December case' that was expected to 'sate' the readers' interest.[17] Many of the papers alerted the public to forthcoming cases. For instance, the *Cork Constitution* noted in 1851 an upcoming case that,

> according to the gossip of the courts, is likely to present more than the usual amount of interest excited in such cases. The fair plaintiff is said to be one of the most engaging of our city belles and the defendant, a wealthy captain in a marching regiment ... damages are laid at £3,000. The letters of the defendant, who moved among society of the highest families in the counties of Cork and Limerick will, it is said, afford no small amount of fun.[18]

2. Limerick stories

Examining a particular set of breach of promise cases allows us see in some detail how women negotiated womanhood, femininity and respectability. It also allows us glimpses of how men presented masculinity and honour. The specific local circumstances of each case help us to understand the changes in cultural and social practices around ideas of courtship, respectability, masculinity and femininity in this period. Exploring individual cases in detail, and looking at the context and circumstances of each case also allows us to see more clearly the considerations that went into the jury's verdicts. The cases investigated in detail in this chapter all derive from the county of Limerick.

In the newspaper reports many of the pre-1830s cases relating to Limerick offer little detail about the plaintiffs or defendants and are often summaries of awards made.[1] A case, reported in unusual detail in 1810, clarifies a breach of promise to marry as a breach of a civil contract. In other words jurists looked on breaches of promise to marry as a breach of contract where a plaintiff could seek redress in a court of law, and could be compensated for the damage done. In this case which involved a rape, the action it was claimed, 'is not only a breach of civil contract, but is a breach of a moral duty, accompanied by the most infamous conduct, followed up by irredeemable ruin'. In order to win their cases lawyers did not hesitate to exaggerate, or play to the jury to elicit .its sympathy for their client. Following the trope that would become the standard means of presenting a plaintiff, this young woman was 22 years of age, described as being from a respectable family, 'her reputation unsullied, her character spotless'. The defendant was deemed to possess 'engaging manners', and had a position with the revenue, though it was also claimed that he was independently wealthy.

The couple appeared well matched. He was introduced to the plaintiff by a Mrs Hunt; very soon he declared he wanted to marry her and said he would talk to her parents, which he did not do. Thus the lawyer was making clear that from the start this was a dishonourable man. From here the story evolves into the melodrama that was to be the standard story of the 'seduced' or 'fallen' woman of the period, though this one ends a little more happily. The couple were in the habit of walking together along the Shannon accompanied by the plaintiff's sister and a Mr Leonard. One afternoon when they were walking, the plaintiff's sister became tired and she and Mr Leonard sat by the river. The couple continued on their walk 'talking of their affection for each other' and then he 'tript [sic] her down, her screams not heard, and she fell a victim not to the passions of a man, but to the fury of a satyr'. Taking on the figure of a beast and losing his humanity the defendant had now immediately lost credibility. Given her passivity and her femininity it was impossible for this woman to prosecute for rape. The plaintiff's lawyer asked, 'Is it for a girl of her education to be the vulgar prosecutrix of a rape, by which the defendant would be elevated to that gallows he deserved'. This she could not do. In the immediate aftermath of the assault her assailant calmed her down and 'spoke of this violence as the anticipation of the rights of a husband'. She became pregnant and he still promised to marry her. No doubt to retain their respectability the woman was soon forced to leave her parent's home and the defendant set her up in 'a hovel at 4s. and 4d. per week' where she lived under the assumed name of Mrs Mahon, never leaving the house. In 1808 she gave birth to a daughter. She met with the defendant's mother who said marriage was impossible. His mother said she would allow the girl 20 guineas per annum but suggested she might enter a Magdalen asylum. The plaintiff did not want to do this and she tried to keep herself by pawning what goods she had. Suggesting that this young woman had some support system in place it was revealed that she relied on the charity of some friends but left one house when it was suggested her child be placed in the Foundling hospital. In the meantime, the defendant had married someone else.

Witnesses, relatives and servants at the trial spoke of seeing the plaintiff and defendant together, of them kissing; there seemed little doubt that a promise to marry had been made. The report of the case is discreet and does not mention the young woman's name and the case was taken for the plaintiff by her father, Christian Sargent. The defendant was clearly identified as James Spring. The fact that she had someone to take a case for her saved her possibly from the fate of many seduced and abandoned women of the period, some of whom ended up earning their living as prostitutes. In this case the jury believed that a contract of marriage had been made and substantial damages of £500 plus costs were awarded. Such an amount was intended to punish the defendant, but also it allowed the plaintiff to live a self-sufficient life.[2] This out of wedlock pregnancy did, initially, separate the woman from her family, and it seems to have taken a number of years before they would see her again. The case for the defence was not strong and there was some mild attempt to disparage the character of the plaintiff by having a witness state he had kissed her at one time. However, such tactics rarely went down well with juries. The reporting of the case left little doubt as to the character of the defendant and the jury quickly came to their decision in support of the plaintiff.

Breach of promise cases are full of human frailty, weakness, manipulation, calculation, ambition as well as evidencing love and attachment, even if only for a short period. In 1869 the case of Emma Bickley and James Murray reveals more about an ambitious young man and his aspirations for business than his desire to marry. This story also gives us an insight into the ways in which women played a significant role in the economic life of the family, and the importance of manufacturing in the economy. Bickley's father was a foreman in the shoemaking department of Cannock and White's, Dublin. James Murray, the defendant, was a traveller or buyer for Cannock, Tait and Co., Limerick. The same partner ran both companies and the staff were well acquainted with each other which was how the couple met. The defendant noted he 'had been struck by her *mien* on a former occasion'. In the summer of 1866, he told her father he had found her employment in Limerick. He was opening a business himself and she 'would do very well for work'. Her family objected as they did not want her to leave Dublin, they would lose the 'advantage to them' as she was very clever at 'flower work' (she was a flowering machinist). Making a decision that suited the family and was advantageous to it, it was decided that the father and daughter would go to work for the defendant, he at 30s. a week and she at 14s. They left the mother behind in Dublin with three sewing machines. In Limerick, the father worked in one room and his daughter mostly in another. 'Of course', as the plaintiff's barrister noted, 'no flirtation could be carried on in the presence of the father and so it was arranged that "when the cats were away, the mice might play"'. Within a fortnight, Murray proposed and she referred him to her father, who consented to the match. They made plans to marry and she brought her family down from Dublin, sewing machines and all. The defendant paid the mother's remaining rent so she could leave Dublin. After a few weeks Bickley, who taught apprentices in this new business, wrote a letter to the father of one of the working girls claiming that she was idle. The defendant, it was claimed, deciding she could not deal with the workers thought it best not to marry her. The next morning her father found two of their sewing machines on the street and he realized he had been evicted. Her father testified that he needed his daughter's expertise or he could not carry out his orders for the shoe shops. The defendant, it was claimed, had profits of £20 a week, a staff of 40–50 in the factory, and £4,000 worth of stock. The family left Limerick and returned to Dublin and the defendant kept one of the sewing machines for the £7 rent he had paid on the mother's behalf. Bickley's mother testified that Murray had come to her in Dublin and asked her consent for marriage, which she gave, but said there was no fortune. He claimed he did not want money, but a 'person who would mind her work'. She took her daughter out of his work when the marriage was not forthcoming. The defence argued that the relationship was all about business and a marriage was never intended.[3]

What makes this case interesting is that the jury did not punish the defendant too severely. There was no doubt that he had a considerable business, that he had persuaded Bickley to work with him, propriety being maintained by the presence of her father, and that he was keener on establishing a good business than he was on marriage. His defence was that he had never made the promise and if he were to marry he would want to have his business set on a solid foundation in order to support a family. The jury was sympathetic to Murray's ambition and perhaps recognizing that Emma could earn her own living, awarded £40 damages and 6*d.* costs.

All kinds of difficulties could, and did, present themselves to intending marriage partners. In breach of promise cases defendants often lost interest in plaintiffs and married someone else, even when a courtship had gone on for a long time. Less often the plaintiff lost interest in the defendant and married someone else. Some men used the promise of marriage as a means of persuading women into a sexual relationship, and then abandoned them months or even years later. Sometimes families interfered and parental permission for the marriage was not granted or relatives, siblings, or children disapproved of the marriage because of a fear they might lose out in some way in relation to an inheritance or perhaps in emotional affection. All of the stories presented by the barristers in court were expected to present their client in the most positive light. Defendants had to provide what appeared to be valid reasons for not proceeding with a marriage. In the following case the existence of a large number of children offered a possible exit strategy for the defendant.

Mary St Lawrence, a 'woman of prepossessing appearance', was the daughter of a respectable hat manufacturer in Limerick, while Michael Skehan, left a widower after 30 years marriage, had property in Co. Clare, had lived in Australia, and was the father of five sons and eight daughters. The eldest daughter was 22 and looked after the children. Another daughter was married but lived with the defendant, whose youngest child was three. He began to court Mary, her family was aware of the relationship; he proposed and the proposal was acceptable to her family. He did make a number of conditions; he wanted to settle two of his sons first. When that was done he later made an excuse that he could not marry while his unmarried daughter lived in the house. A number of letters were read out in court and it was evident that there was some local gossip about their relationship. He told Mary to ignore it, 'do not mind', he wrote, 'what other folks say; treat them with contempt, and let them guess about what is to come on, and it will be a mystery to them when and where we will spend the honeymoon'. The gossip continued and he advised Mary to 'hold up your head, and be independent to them; let them be talking, and let us be happy'. Skehan had not, apparently, told his children of his impending marriage and they learned of it from a neighbour. Mary claimed that his daughter did not want the marriage to happen and he responded, 'I always told you I would never bring in a wife while Norah [his daughter] was a mother over my own children. You said to me that you should be a mistress of your own house if you married.' Then suddenly he proposed and Mary asked for a month to 'consider and to consult my friends', but he, clearly wanting to put some pressure on her, would only give her a fortnight. The marriage was then arranged. He had originally stated that he had an income of £600 a year, but then said he had £400. In court she was asked if she knew that he was old enough to be her father and she claimed she did not know what age he was.

In his evidence Skehan noted that he was paralyzed in one leg and could not work and had an income of £300. Claiming illness was a common ploy on the part of defendants to justify their not following through on a marriage proposal. The couple met, he stated, on the station platform at Limerick going to Killaloe. She was with a Mrs Hare and it was Mrs Hare who suggested the marriage. He then met her in Mrs Hare's house in Killaloe and proposed. 'I had previously', he said, 'never said anything soft to her, or thrown sheep's eyes at her'. He told Mary he could not marry for twelve months on account of his children and he needed to marry off his eldest two daughters. He claimed that he gave Mary money on every visit, a practice that implied a plaintiff's bad character, and also claimed he had given money to every member of the family, amounting to £300 to £400. Despite Skehan's very large family he did not convince the jury that the delay in carrying through the marriage was excusable and they awarded the plaintiff £100.[4] Younger women courting older men was a common enough occurrence in these court cases but one always noted by lawyers as laughable and somehow unnatural. Juries recognized that older men often had considerable wealth and this was understood and accepted as a pragmatic transaction.

The case of Elizabeth Sheehy *v.* John Evans O'Leary, with damages claimed at £5,000 excited much interest in Limerick in 1873. Elizabeth was from a respectable Limerick family, the daughter of Mr Roger Keatinge Sheehy, JP, a landed proprietor, while the defendant was a gentleman from Fort Shannon, Glin, Co. Limerick, an officer in the Limerick Militia and nephew of the late General Sir De Lacy Evans, MP. The couple had first met in June 1865, and she often then met him at her father's house. Elizabeth, aged 26, had received about 149 letters from the defendant, and she wrote him just as many. O'Leary made his feelings for her plain from the very first letter where he declared,

> My own Darling Betty, I don't know how to begin my first letter to you, but I believe the best way is to say that there is not in the world a man that loves another as I love you. I will love you as long as I live, and just as sincerely and devotedly as I do now to the day of my death. Will you be the same to me, my own heart?

His letters to her continued in that vein and he often signed himself 'husband' and asked her to sign herself 'wife', which she did occasionally. Some of his letters reveal his jealousy of her and there are suggestions that she accused him

of being unfaithful to her. The defendant had property of between £10,000
and £12,000 under his uncle's will. He proposed to Elizabeth in 1865 and she
said she would consent to marry him if she had her father's permission, which
was forthcoming.

O'Leary then began to lose interest and wrote less frequently to her in 1868
and 1869, but begged her to trust him. He gave her a ring before his uncle
died, which caused trouble with his cousin. In 1871 he visited her regularly
and came to her father's house and it was then she observed a 'change in his
manner' towards her. Showing their closeness she remarked that 'he always
called me by my Christian name, and I called him by his'. In cross examination,
and in questioning other witnesses, it appears that O'Leary had a drink
problem and had at one stage taken the pledge. O'Leary's financial circumstances were detailed in the court and it appeared he had £240 a year and
about £1,140 in cash. The jury found for the plaintiff and awarded her a
substantial £1,875.[5]

A newspaper commentary made following the trial noted that in one of
her letters read out in court Elizabeth had alluded to a forthcoming breach of
promise case in Dublin. 'Damages', she wrote, 'are laid at £4,000. If she gets
£1,000 I suppose it will be the most. I don't think it right for any lady to
bring an action, although it is the only way for a young lady to make any
money'. That women deliberately brought breach of promise cases in order to
make money was a public concern at the time. However, at least in this
commentary it was argued that the damages awarded in such cases were rarely
excessive and in fact that the male defendants did better out of it than the
plaintiffs.[6]

As this study illustrates social attitudes to sexuality were perhaps still a little
more fluid in the late 19th century than we are accustomed to believe. While
the local clergy might not be able to force people to give up inappropriate
relationships they could refuse to marry the couple in order to effect the
outcome they believed most moral. Mary Fox a young 'country girl' from
Galbally, Co. Limerick, was the third daughter, and one of five children, of a
man who farmed 30 acres, near Kilfinane. The defendant, James Roche, had a
'substantial farm' in the same area, which gave him an income of about £80
a year. Mary's aunt and uncle had a dairy farm that they had taken from Roche
and the plaintiff and defendant used to meet there. This was typical of rural
courtship where couples found it difficult to secure privacy. A considerable
amount of intimacy seems to have taken place in fields and farm out-buildings.
The couple eventually became engaged but prior to the engagement, the
defendant had been linked with a Miss Condon with whom he had a child,
although he denied paternity. The local clergyman, 'having regard to the morals
of the parish', objected to the engagement of Roche and Fox and refused to
perform a marriage until something should be done for Miss Condon. The
couple then decided to go to Cork to get married, but the clergyman there

refused to perform the ceremony without some references from the priest of their own parish. Then Roche went to a solicitor and deeded all his disposable property and all interest in his farm to Fox *in lieu* of marriage. If anything should invalidate that deed then she was to be compensated with £500 cash. They then asked the archbishop of Cashel to allow them to marry but he refused to interfere. At this point Roche married Miss Condon. Mary Fox, as a result of the deed, took possession of Roche's land and house in Ballybrian, and it was reported in court that after the marriage, Roche, his new wife and the plaintiff lived together in the house for about a month 'in a sort of armed neutrality'. Mary Fox stated that 'she did not speak to Mary Condon' when she was in the house: 'we used not to cook our food on the same fire. We used often meet during the day, but we never sat down to the fire together in the evening'. There was overwhelming evidence that Roche had made a promise of marriage to Fox but the jury only awarded her £60 damages rather than the £500 sought. It is not clear from the evidence available whether she left the farm and land to Roche and his new wife, or how that arrangement carried on. She may very well still have been in possession and hence the low award of £60.[7] It is difficult to know what the jury was compensating in this case. Roche was believed to be a bit of a hothead, but in marrying Condon the mother of his child, he had, in fact, done the 'manly' thing. It is likely that the jury were literally assessing damages for the actual breach of promise, which had been proven to exist, but juries had awarded amounts lower than £60 in many such cases. Perhaps because the woman's father had 30 acres, £60 was deemed a more suitable award.

Margaret Grace, aged 28, sued Christopher O'Brien, a widowed farmer, aged 40, from Pallasgreen, Co. Limerick, for breach of promise and seduction. She was employed as a barmaid in Pallasgreen in 1909 and came to know the defendant while she worked there. He became attached to her and visited regularly, sometimes twice a day. Grace had kept a record of their meetings and she provided the court with the dates and places where 'misconduct' took place. After a while a marriage date was fixed, the wedding breakfast ordered and £200 was to be paid to the defendant on the day before the wedding. However, the defendant would accept nothing less than £250 and the engagement was called off. Grace then had a baby and O'Brien agreed to support it. The facts of the case are laid out very clearly in the newspaper report and no comments are made about immorality or the 'blighted' prospects of the plaintiff. This language was certainly a feature of the period when discussing unmarried mothers, a subject of much public concern at this time, but no judgement is made on the woman's morality in this case. The jury awarded the plaintiff £300.[8]

The final case is unusual both in Limerick and in Ireland in that the plaintiff was a man. William Tarvener, a sea captain, sued Miss Elizabeth Sullivan, of Killmallock, for breach of promise seeking £500 damages. The defendant declared she was under no liability to the plaintiff and brought six pence into court to 'satisfy the plaintiff's claim'. This case was also unusual in that it involved religious differences. The plaintiff was a Protestant and the defendant a Catholic and in order for them to marry the defendant needed a dispensation. The judge made it clear that the requirements of the Catholic church did not mean they had to be taken note of in the court. While the defendant's barrister sought to use the need for a dispensation as the reason why the couple had not married, the judge stressed that he would hear no arguments relating to Canon law. However, the judge did state that he would explain to the jury that her letters to the plaintiff stated that she could not marry him without a dispensation. The defence made much of the need for this dispensation and in typical fashion mocked the male plaintiff for taking the case at all. The plaintiff's barrister declared that there was 'much religion and politics in this country' but that in the 'jury box there was neither politics nor religion'. He argued that a contract had been made and it was binding under the law of the land. He stated 'there was talk about these actions being brought against women. Women and men had the same rights under civil law. Women were now invading the professions of the men. They were competing with them in various employments. They had begun even to take men's bicycles'. If women wanted all of these options then they must also face the consequences of their actions. The judge put a simple question to the jury, did the plaintiff have any right to damages? The jury was unable to come to a decision after more than two hours deliberation. At one stage they did ask the judge what was the smallest amount that would carry costs, which suggests that while they had sympathy for the plaintiff he was not going to get any financial reward for his case. In the end nothing was agreed and the judge believed that the issue of religion had made it impossible for the jury to agree on a verdict.[9]

The language of the courts and the ways in which breach of promise cases were reported changed subtly by the end of the 19th century. Whatever rhetorical devices barristers had used over the decades had either diminished considerably or were not reported in the papers. The 'sensational' aspects of the cases were no longer highlighted. They became very matter-of-fact in their reportage. Women were still expected to be virtuous and respectable when appearing in court, and men were expected to be considerate and manly in their defence. These cases were essentially about people who had changed their minds, realized they had made mistakes, or felt compelled by circumstances to agree to marriages they did not necessarily desire. Breach of promise cases also reveal society's expectation that women should marry, a belief echoed perhaps in the success women had as plaintiffs in these cases.

3. Courtship

There are many commonalities between breach of promise cases that were taken around the country and those that relate directly to Limerick city and county and these help to provde the context within which to understand the Limerick stories. There is a similarity about all breach of promise cases in terms of their narrative and exposition in the courts. The stories told in court were pretty standard and perhaps expected by the jury; the injured and wronged woman facing the dishonourable man, not for financial gain but to reinforce her respectability in a public setting. In this and the following chapter the wider social, economic and legal contexts of the Limerick stories will be analyzed by reference to cases elsewhere in Ireland to help our understanding of the world of Limerick.

Evidence presented in breach of promise cases tells us a considerable amount about how couples met and courted in this period. In Frost's study of breach of promise cases, 42 per cent of the couples in her sample met through friends, relatives, or knew each other as neighbours; 27 per cent met in the workplace, including defendants who might have employed the plaintiff; 14 per cent met at balls, picnics, or church-related activities and 6 per cent first knew each other through a landlord-tenant relationship. About 11 per cent met as strangers, or through matchmaking.[1] It is not yet possible to quantify how the couples in the Irish cases met, though it is clear that matchmaking was an element in arranging meetings in the post-Famine period. Couples met in similar ways to Frost's sample, through family gatherings, at dances, through friends and family. At the lower levels of society they met in public houses, at fairs, or on the streets. Anne Carroll, a parlourmaid, met James Farrelly, who worked for his father in their own grocer's business, on her way home from Mass in 1873.[2] Mary Dwyer worked as a general servant for Samuel Reali, before he seduced her under a promise of marriage.[3] From the evidence available servants who had relationships with their employers were more likely to have had sex with the defendant, or at least this is made more evident in the court proceedings. Rebecca Hodgens met William Brooke Beatty at the theatre. They left the theatre together and he took her to a hotel where they had champagne and then they went to a house in Dublin, and lived together as man and wife for about seven years.[4] Mary Blakeney, only daughter of the late James Blakeney, crown solicitor for Co. Galway, met Henry Gribbon Byrne, an engineer 'of means and independence' at a ball in Dublin. They danced two or three times that night.

Afterwards he accompanied her home from church and 'fondly addressed her' so that she eventually introduced him to her mother. He subsequently visited her regularly at the house.[5] Rowena Chute met John Du Bouley Blennerhassett, 'staffed in that school of gallantry, the army', and then a JP and with property worth £800 a year, at a ball.[6] In the Co. Cork case of Heard *v.* Longfield the defendant asked to meet the plaintiff when he had heard her playing music in a friend's house.[7]

That the permission of parents or guardians was expected in all marriage proposals comes out strongly in these breach of promise cases. Often the refusal of a parent or guardian to support an alliance was used by the defendant to argue for the breach of promise and defendants expected sympathy from the jury on this score. The fact that parents were not aware of the courtship was also used as a defence. Eliza Moore sued James Thompson in 1841 and the defence noted that damages should be less than requested as the couple kept the courtship secret from their families.[8] Marianne Delany's father refused the visits of her suitor until his aunt approved of the match. [9] Anne Corish sued Richard Codd, both from prosperous farming backgrounds in Co. Wexford, for breach of promise in 1850. In this instance the defence claimed that the marriage was conditional on his father's consent, which was not forthcoming.[10] Maryanne Griott and Robert Ryan had courted for 17 years. Here the defendant's father objected to the match and had arranged another for his son, which the son refused.[11] While Ryan's relationship with Griott later disintegrated he was, like some other offspring of the period, unwilling to take the partner chosen for him. This sometimes led to children losing out on an inheritance. Adult offspring did object to parents remarrying as was the case in O'Hanlon *v.* Ryan, both from Limerick, where the defendant declared that he had informed the plaintiff he would not marry her without the support of his children.[12] Sometimes young, unmarried women kept house for their widowed father and were unhappy to have their position usurped by a bride. Others feared that their share of the inheritance would be diminished.

COURTING

Courtship was recognized as a stage in the marriage process, it involved certain rituals that allowed a couple to get to know each other. Courtship practices were investigated by both plaintiffs' and defendants' lawyers in court. The length of courtship, long or short, could influence the jury in assessing damages. Where and how couples met, whether they saw each other alone, the physical contact they had, and the knowledge their families or communities had of the courtship were all issues addressed in evidence. Feelings and emotions were elicited from the plaintiff and defendant when they could provide their own evidence from 1869. While it is impossible to generalize about the norms of courtship from the cases under review, it is possible to get a sense of accepted ways of behaving and the meaning of that behaviour in the process of courtship.

In 1819 in Berwick *v.* Cyrne the details of the courtship, supported by witness testimony, helped win damages for the plaintiff. Elizabeth Berwick owned a school in Dun Laoghaire and the defendant was a butcher who lived in the same place. It was argued that he saw a match there as something that would 'promote his domestic happiness' but also help his business. It was reported that he 'continually sought her company … and in fact the whole village had long laid down that the marriage would soon take place, as they were inseparable'. Witnesses reported that the couple went together to chapel every Sunday in the same vehicle, and knelt together side by side. Another witness testified that when he passed Berwick's house once he saw the defendant mending the bolt on a window shutter. The jury clearly believed from this evidence that a promise to marry had been made and awarded the plaintiff £40 damages and 6*d.* costs.[13] Although we have no intimate details of this courtship, for the local population the ways in which this couple presented themselves in public, attending chapel together, the act of house maintenance, signaled an inevitable marriage. Likewise in the Dublin case of Delany *v.* McGarry, the plaintiff's sister testified that the defendant had known the plaintiff for seven years and that 'he was on intimate terms with the family'. 'He brought us', she said, 'to concerts and to a circus, and also on parties of pleasure'. He had also given the plaintiff presents of bouquets, gloves and a gold watch. After a dinner party he had danced all evening with the plaintiff.[14] Again in Dublin in 1863 it was noted that in the Tallon *v.* Hassard case the defendant had sent the plaintiff a 'valentine ornamented with a true lover's knot and pretty sketch of a church with a man and woman linking arms'.[15]

In Flynn *v.* Kiernan, both from farming communities in Co. Kildare, the defendant had asked if he could go on a trip with a friend and a number of his female relatives. He wished to be introduced to one of the women. At the railway he was asked which of the girls he wanted to be introduced to and he noted it was Eliza Flynn. They all went off on the trip and in the train on the way back the couple had 'one side of the car to themselves, and had a cloak covering them'. This was seen and understood in the court as an intimate gesture and caused much laughter. The defendant came home with the plaintiff's family in their car. On the following Sunday he visited again and then came on a number of evenings. Her fortune was to be £50 and she agreed to be married to him.[16] Courtships were signaled by suitors being known to the family, giving presents and tokens to their loved one and frequent visits.

In 1860, Marianne Delany, 19, the convent-educated daughter of a Dublin pawnbroker sued John McGarry, who was heir to his father's business.

Reflecting the social standing of the couples damages of £5,000 were sought. She was about 13, and he 16 or 17 when they met at friends' houses and often 'rambled together among the groves'. Over time they fell in love and he paid her addresses throughout her youth, visiting her when she stayed with friends and even made an unsuccessful attempt to see her in the convent. He lived with an aunt and uncle who disapproved of the relationship, but after his uncle died, he again pursued her. One evening they had dinner at a mutual friend's house, they danced a quadrille afterwards and he proposed. She accepted on the condition that her parents consented and, in a novelistic rendering of the scene, the reporter noted 'they walked home together, in the moonlight', after the dance.[17] In Newton *v*. Mungavin the plaintiff owned a general draper's shop in Dun Laoghaire, while Mungavin was retired from the Indian army and aged at least 76. Newton was about 48 years old. Their courtship centered around the shop where he had an account for his daughter and grandchildren. He called frequently, and had lunch and tea there.[18]

Another defendant, James Cassidy, who ran a public house in Dublin, gave precise details about his courtship. He testified that he knew the plaintiff for ten years and courted her until 1892 and they were engaged. He saw her twice on Sundays, 12.30–1.30 and 8.30–11p.m., and then a couple of times during the week. In the day, he saw her in his father's shop and at night he would meet her there and go out, weather permitting; if bad, they retired to the house and played cards or some other amusement. Over the courtship, she gave him small presents, including a rosary and beads, but he did not return these when the relationship ended. He also received a plait of her hair 'to wear next to your heart'.[19] Giving presents was a common practice, and included rings, which was taken by juries to mean a marriage had been proposed, and brooches, books, and other articles, and by the end of the century photographs.[20] Gifts were expected to be returned if the relationship broke down. In Henry *v*. McCarrick the defence noted that no presents, or gifts had been exchanged by the couple and there was very little evidence of them spending time together. A proposal of marriage had been made in January 1861 and by July of the same year the matter had come to court.[21] In Dublin in 1863 in Plunkett *v*. Muldoon, the plaintiff felt she had enough evidence for a court case though no one had witnessed the marriage proposal. She testified that 'he escorted me to the theatre, and he walked out with me, and my name is in the mouths of people, and I have grounds enough'.[22]

In Fitzpatrick *v*. Vint, both from, Co. Antrim, the defendant declared when she informed him she had no fortune, 'Mary we'll marry for love and then work for the riches'. He was a constant visitor and accepted suitor by her family. The couple were accustomed to sitting up after everyone else had gone to bed and on one such occasion, he succeeded in seducing the plaintiff.[23] In many of the cases the couples were left alone together and this seems to have been standard practice in all classes. In Millan *v.* McConnell the courtship continued for twelve years with the defendant stating he had not the means to support a wife. A month before the court case he married someone else.[24] In Brennan *v.* Meade the defendant had sent the plaintiff pocket handkerchiefs for Christmas on which was written in marking ink 'from one who loves you well'.[25]

Once a relationship was known to exist couples literally went walking together, the man visited the family, and took meals with them. In Tallon *v.* Hassard, the mother testified that he took 'all his meals at her house'.[26] In Plunkett *v.* Muldoon the defendant became a regular visitor to the house, staying for several hours at a time.[27] In a case from 1872 it was noted that the defendant 'was unceasing in calling for weeks' to the plaintiff's home.[28] Likewise the relationship between Lucy Fitzgerald and a surgeon named Fox commenced when he attended an 'evening party' given by her father in Dublin. When the plaintiff's family went to live in Kilkee the defendant 'dined with them on two or three occasions'. After a while he cooled towards her and the relationship ended. Miss Fitzgerald 'declined on several occasions to go to evening amusements, concerts, etc.,' because he did not wish to go with her.[29] Donogh O'Brien visited the family of Dorothea Forrest 'daily'.[30] In the case of Head *v.* Purdon the defendant lived a mile from the plaintiff's father's house. The couple courted for eight years. Letters and gifts were exchanged though the defence argued that it was not a real courtship as the families, though living so close never visited each other.[31]

There were times when the courtship was sudden and the promise made in haste. Samuel Brigell, a farmer and a widower from Co. Derry, had asked to be introduced to the plaintiff Annabella McKee, having declared 'that he gone over the best of all the eligible girls, but the plaintiff was the only girl in the world for him.' He offered her marriage at their first meeting, but she said it was too soon and she needed time. He called again a short time later and she agreed to marry and they organized the wedding for 7 January. The courtship had essentially lasted two weeks. James Getty testified to making the introduction and then 'he discreetly withdrew, leaving them alone.' It was revealed that Brignell kissed McKee at every meeting. The plaintiff on being asked 'Was there any violent love-making?' stated, 'Oh, he passed himself very well, indeed.' He then told her he was too nervous to get married and postponed the wedding but he married someone else on Easter Sunday. When asked about her £1,000 claim for damages she stated, much to the amusement of the court, 'that man could court as much in a fortnight as another man would in five years.' She sent her engagement presents back. The jury in this case awarded £72 10*s*.[32] In Darker *v.* Sparrow the defence argued that this was not a story of romance, but of a girl who wanted to get married and failed in her object. The defendant claimed that she wanted to marry a fortnight after they met and the barrister observed that 'this was fast enough, even in this age of electricity' but that it was really just 'courtship, flirtation, kissing and fun', not a courtship in expectation of marriage. The judge noted that the plaintiff was from a respectable family and would not allowed herself to be kissed by the defendant unless there had been a promise of marriage. The jury agreed and awarded her £250.[33]

The witnessing of physical touch, whether it was kissing, which appears to have the most intimate act to perform in public, or sitting on someone's knee, was used by barristers as clear evidence that a relationship existed between a couple. In Harris *v.* Boyd the defendant acknowledged that the plaintiff often sat on his knee.[34] Catherine Murphy and James Walsh, both from Co. Limerick, had known each other for 15 years and when he proposed and she agreed to marry him, he 'shook her by the hand and kissed her, and said she was as much his wife as if they had stood before a priest'. She told the court that he had 'come in once and sent in for me and wanted to kiss me. I said the priest would kill me if I allowed him, and he said was I not his own, and I said I could not let him.'[35] This occurred in the early 1870s and the couple were still in their teens, which might explain the response of the girl to his attempt to kiss her. In O'Dwyer *v.* Maguire the defendant denied ever kissing the plaintiff.[36] In O'Hanlon *v.* Ryan the plaintiff was asked by her barrister if Ryan, a town councillor in Limerick city, had kissed her, she hesitated before answering yes and the barrister immediately made it clear to the court that since the couple were engaged this was a perfectly respectable thing to have done.[37]

RELIGION

Religion does not seem to have been a major factor in any of these breach of promise cases. At times Catholic priests did attempt to intervene. The parish priest in Ballitore, Co. Kildare, wrote to Cardinal Cullen in 1875 about an attempt to stop a breach of promise getting to the courts. The man involved told him that,

> he was determined to defend any action rather than marry his cousin. At the same time he expresses his willingness to give her what I consider a very fair sum to forego all legal proceedings and thus avoid very painful outcomes[?] She is still staying in this parish with a person, who is no relative, I saw her and suggested to her the propriety of accepting a sum of money to enable her to emigrate and hide her shame in a foreign country. But she refused in such a manner as to make me think she has little sense of shame left. Father McDonnell C.C. of Baltinglass has been written to to ask him to influence her brother to put a stop to proceedings. I hope this step may be successful in getting rid of a very nasty affair.[38]

However, this case did come to court and the evidence given makes it clear that Anne Lennon had been seduced by the defendant and an 'improper intimacy existed for several years' between them. She became pregnant and left the area to have the child, who died. They continued their relationship after the child's death. She was unsure of her age but believed she was 35 years old. The defendant's barrister stated that at that age she was old enough to know better than engage in a relationship of this nature. The defendant told her they were cousins and it would be a disgrace if they married. The judge said the defendant's story 'was one of the most improbable that had ever been introduced in a court of justice. Nothing could be more improbable than that the plaintiff, who had been in this intimate relationship with this man for three years, should not wish him to marry her.' It was reported that the judge 'said nothing on the question of morality; the less said about that the better.' He directed the jury to find for the plaintiff but not to give punitive damages, but damages that would compensate her. They awarded £600 and 6d. costs.[39] In another case from Kildare a priest sought a speedy dispensation for a Mr Wall who had been served with a writ for breach of promise. He was being sued for £2,000 because of the delay in proceeding with the marriage.[40]

Sometimes issues of conversion came up in these cases. In Roundtree *v.* Lee in 1857 it was alleged that the plaintiff, who was a Catholic, had promised the defendant that she would become a Protestant. The plaintiff was 17 years old and the defendant about 35 years old. Her stepmother, who gave evidence in court, stated that the defendant had started to pay attention to the plaintiff when she was 12 years old. When Mary was 16 he suggested to the stepmother that he might marry her. The stepmother felt said she was too young and also needed assurance that he would not interfere with her religion. He said he would not and the marriage date was set. Clothes were bought and the 'young girl was the talk of the country and town'. Then he came to break off the match saying his friends very much opposed it. The stepmother said it was too late, that money had been spent and that the girl 'had been talked about'. He claimed that he had discovered that by his father's will he would lose £200 a year if he married a Catholic. If the girl went with him to Church for a while then he would marry her. If not, he offered £50 as 'compensation and to get a husband'. The stepmother told him that 'husbands were not to be bought or sold in Monasterevan'. When asked by the defence barrister if she knew that Archbishop Cullen had prohibited mixed marriages in the diocese she swore she had not been aware of the fact. The Protestant minister said he would prefer it if she married someone of her own religion but that if she did go to church for a few days it 'would be only a nine-day wonder'. Contradictory evidence was provided by witnesses as to whether the girl was to convert or not. When the marriage was called off that was no longer an issue. The jury awarded her £60 in damages.[41] Likewise, Miss Van Esbeck of Limerick, sought to recover damages of £5,000 from the eldest son of

Christopher John Delmege, JP. The marriage had been postponed to allow
Delmege time to convert to Catholicism. But he then left the country on the
urging, it was alleged, of his family who 'took him by the neck in order to
coerce him' and he went to America.[42]

In 1861 in McBarron v. Dixon the defendant, who was Protestant from Co.
Tyrone, had asked the plaintiff's father to arrange with the Catholic priest to
marry them but he refused, though the priest did promise to read the religious
service if the marriage was first performed by a registrar.[43] In 1847 Margaret
Goodwin, from Ballymena, sued William Holden for breach of promise and
sought £200 damages. It transpired that the plaintiff was a Catholic and the
defendant a Presbyterian. Her barrister addressed the jury stating 'you know
the feeling which is prevalent among Presbyterians against marriages between
protestants and Roman Catholics. It is a feeling founded upon the idea that
religious difference but too often create disquiet in families, and destroy the
harmony which is so essential to the happiness of married life'. In 1836 the
defendant promised he would marry the plaintiff when he could. They began
a sexual relationship and had two children together. The defendant tried to
get married but his parents refused their consent and none of the local clergy
would marry them without it. He then joined the constabulary and was moved
away from the plaintiff to Co. Louth. He corresponded with her for two years
and then when he returned home in 1845 he married someone else, who
brought some property as a dowry. The defence barrister argued that Goodwin
had 'artfully contrived the whole scheme for the purpose of extorting money
from the defendant'. The jury awarded the plaintiff £20 in damages and 6d.
costs.[44] It is probable that religion does not surface as an issue in these cases
because most couples were of the same religion. What does become obvious,
and this will be discussed later, is that the Catholic church, while it seemed
unable in many instances to compel couples in irregular unions to separate,
exerted its power by refusing to marry these couples when they sought to do
so. This refusal sometimes led to the break up of the relationship.[45]

FORTUNES

While we know that dowries were very much part of the marriage system in
post-Famine Ireland, and to a lesser extent in pre-Famine Ireland, we still do
not have a comprehensive understanding of how dowries were used, or the
value of dowries over time in different parts of Ireland and in relation to
different classes.[46] What is clear from looking at the breach of promise cases is
that a dowry, or fortune, was expected in marriages after the 1850s. Lack of a
dowry, or what was believed to be an insufficient dowry, was used by
defendants as a reason to break off a proposal of marriage. It is evident from

the cases reviewed that juries expected dowries to be part of the marriage 'package', though they were sympathetic to plaintiffs where the amount of the dowry was questioned by defendants. Looking specifically at match-making and dowries tells us a lot about how families were constructed in this period, about the use of material resources in a household, about status, about the place of women and men in households, about power relationships and, of course, about the importance and value of land in Irish farming families. These issues were as significant in Limerick as they were in other Irish counties. Dowries were so common by the 1860s that in one case the judge admonished a defendant for not inquiring about a woman's fortune, and other 'particulars' before he proposed to her and had discussions with her father. It was too late, he stated, to do so after the event and discover that such matters were unsatisfactory.[47]

James Farrelly told Anne Carroll, very soon after meeting her, that he was in love with her. The pair lived in Bray, Co. Wicklow, and there was correspondence between them amounting to 18 letters. In one letter he inquired after her fortune and she responded that she did not have one and had not the means to acquire one. His letters usually began with 'My dearly loved Annie'. He wrote to ask whether her friends would provide a fortune and then he asked her to come to Dublin and apologized for talking about money. The correspondence ended and he married someone else with a fortune. In court he denied that a promise to marry had been made and said it was conditional on her getting a fortune. He admitted to the jury that 'I was looking for money and that was the reason why I corresponded with the girl'. His father did not know of his courtship. He would have married for £100 or even £50 and he got £50 with his new bride. He admitted to telling the girl he loved her on first meeting her, but 'there was no talk of money then'. The jury awarded the plaintiff £40.[48] In 1892 Bridget O'Connell, the daughter of a farmer near Athea in Co. Limerick, sued Acting Inspector Cregan of the Dublin Metropolitan Police. He claimed that he was to receive £100 as her fortune before the marriage and that it had not been paid, and he was still willing to marry her if the money was forthcoming.[49]

Although men infrequently took breach of promise cases Patrick Quail sued John Murray and his wife Elizabeth in 1852 for breach of promise to marry. The case, no doubt because it was taken by a man, 'excited considerable interest and created much amusement during its progress amongst the vast crowd that filled the court'. Quail was 28 years old, and had a small farm of twenty-five acres in Co. Meath and the woman's father held a farm about the same size in Co. Cavan. Her father had three daughters and it was claimed intended to marry Bridget off 'advantageously… with the least possible expense to himself in the item of her fortune'. The couple met in 1848 at Quail's uncle's house and his wife was a cousin of Bridget's. The couple got on well together, met numerous times and a wedding date was set for 18 August 1851. On the morning of the wedding Quail was informed by his proposed bride's father that the wedding was off and that she now intended to marry John Murray. 'The parties first met in his house, and there was some match-making gone on with; but the matter was deferred to a subsequent meeting, which took place in a public house, in the town of Kingscourt … When the fortune was spoken of the old man offered £50, £25 in hand, and the rest in future payments.' It was claimed by Quail's brother that the father had persuaded her to marry Murray as he was 'richer' than Quail. Quail gave the father a bill for £7 8s. 2d. for the costs he had incurred in preparing for the wedding. Quail won his case and was awarded £25 damages and 6d. costs.[50]

When John McGarry, who had been courting Marianne Delany, decided to marry her he had a cousin formally approach her father for permission. An interview was arranged with him and money was discussed. McGarry had £5,000 (£2,000 in the business and the rest in Scotch securities) and asked for £1,000. Delany, who was a pawnbroker with shops in Dublin, demurred and thinking of his large family of four daughters and one son, offered £700 to McGarry, £300 on the wedding day, £200 two years later and £200 on death. McGarry pressed for £1,000. Delany observed 'you are like a man who was bargaining for a sheep or a cow; is it my daughter you want or is it money?' McGarry still insisted on £1,000 with Delany refusing to go to this amount and after some negotiations with the defendant's solicitor the marriage was broken off. First McGarry claimed to be ill, a common excuse in breach of promise cases, then that he would only go ahead if he got £700 at once. The defendant did not offer any defence in court but had his barrister ask the plaintiff's father to allow him marry his daughter. The father responding through his barrister stated he 'would rather die first'. The jury upheld the plaintiff's case and awarded £500 damages and 6d. costs.[51] One woman, who was the daughter of a prosperous farmer, and married in 1880 articulated the significance of material wealth to the relationship. 'Father came in and gave me his blessing. He cared a great deal for my happiness and thought Richard and I were well suited to one another; besides which Richard's land and prospects were on a par with the dowry he would give with me'.[52] So even when money was the basis of a marriage this did not mean that parents were completely oblivious to the happiness of their children.

Juries also could be sympathetic to expectations that men had of the fortune or dowry that women might bring to a marriage. In 1906 Julia Brannigan, a farmer's daughter, from Brittas in Co. Louth, sued Patrick Howell for £500. He claimed that any promise of marriage was conditional on him receiving £250 as a marriage portion, which, in this case had not been fulfilled. She had a fortune of £200, and claimed he demanded £300 and then reduced the amount to £250. Her brother then offered £225, which the plaintiff claimed the defendant accepted. But the defendant was adamant that he would take no less than £250 needing that amount to pay off his debts. The jury awarded the plaintiff £30, a relatively small amount given the claim made. This award recognizes that the plaintiff had a case but also suggests that it was acceptable for the defendant to demand a substantial dowry.[53]

Juries understood the financial and economic necessity of women to marry, and even where economic motives were blatantly obvious they still allowed substantial damages. In 1897 Catherine Darcy, 'a young lady of prepossessing appearance' and in her early twenties sued Terence Dunne, a man of 'mature age'. It appears that some attempt at match making had occurred in this case. Darcy had only spoken to Dunne once before she, her father, and uncle went to Portumna and met the defendant, his sister, and uncle. They all went into a private room in a public house. The matchmaker, James Quinn, then asked Darcy if she was satisfied with Dunne and she said she was. The defendant then produced a cheque for £450 and asked the plaintiff's father what he would offer as her fortune. Her father suggested £50 but Dunne wanted £60, but then accepted the £50. The wedding date was set, the plaintiff spent £15 on her wedding trousseau. The couple were to go 'half in half with the marriage money', her side were to have 20 guests while the defendant was to have 24. Then she had a letter from the defendant calling off the wedding. In court Darcy admitted Dunne was an old man but that she was willing to marry him. When asked if she were anxious to marry him she replied 'I was'. And when asked why she replied that he 'was well off'. The barrister then asked if it was the £450 she was marrying and she responded she was 'marrying both'. The defendant claimed he broke the engagement because the marriage money had not been paid. However, it appeared that the fortune was to be paid on the morning of the wedding and the defendant had little reason for calling off the engagement. The jury awarded Darcy £100.[54]

Match making was more prevalent in the post-Famine period but it was also evident in the pre-Famine period. Writing in 1839, a Kilkenny man described the nature of the match 'apparently [there is] very little love or sentiment between the interested pair, the whole affair being conducted and concluded by the parents and friends on both sides in quite a businesslike manner, just as they would dispose of their stock or swap a farm'.[55] There were a few official matchmakers, but family members or friends might arrange a match. Sometimes they introduced a couple and sometimes they were also involved in the negotiations around the dowry and settlement to be made.

In Brosnan *v.* Herlihy it was reported that in December 1892 the defendant, from Co. Cork, and some friends proceeded to the plaintiff's house in Farranfore, Co. Kerry, where a match was proposed 'as was the custom of the country'. It was agreed that the defendant should get the plaintiff's father's farm on condition of paying over a sum of money. It was noted that the match making 'went on for some hours', and when the terms were finally agreed upon, the plaintiff's brother said if he did not get £80 for himself no one should come near the farm. On hearing this the defendant broke off the negotiations. The plaintiff claimed that further negotiations began later that year but when all the marriage arrangements were made the defendant did not turn up on the day.[56]

Margaret Driver sued Terence Quin, both of the 'farming class', in 1873 and sought damages of £1,000. The plaintiff resided in Ballymore Eustace. The defendant had been in America but returned when he inherited land from a relative. On his return he proposed to the plaintiff, but after two years of courting he still had not fulfilled his promise, despite a trousseau being purchased. Her lawyer suggested he was after more money. The plaintiff testified that about two or three years before the defendant approached her and said he had been talking to her father about her, and he offered a fortune of £200. Being one of five daughters she believed that was too much to expect from her father. He responded that that was nothing to her as long as her father was willing to give it. She replied it was a fortune he was looking for, not a wife, but he disagreed and proposed marriage, and she consented. He told her they would marry once he built a house on the land her father had given him and got some stock. He also told her she was very innocent not to make him settle £50 a year on her before she put on the rings. He went to buy the rings, and they arranged a priest, bridesmaid and groomsman. She and her mother went to Dublin to buy the dress though he told her not to spend too much. He then did not see her for a while and was angry at her father for sending a letter suggesting he would 'humbug' her. He then fell out with them over the letter. The barrister, when questioning the father, noted he had five daughters and suggested that the defendant picked the pretty one. Her father said he let the defendant please himself as to choice. The father claimed that the defendant was worth about £2,500–£3,000. When they fell out the father heard that the defendant was offered a fortune of £300–£400. The phrasing of this is of course, very interesting, as it is the fortune that is being offered, not a wife. The defence argued it was a pure money match and that there was a 'total absence of heartbreaking emotion', it was claimed also that his family did not approve the match as 'mothers as a rule did not like to see their sons married', and the Driver family were not of an equal social class. The jury awarded £200 damages and 6d. costs.[57]

That marriage was a financial transaction is evident from many of the cases, including those from Limerick. In 1886 Mary Mulvihille, formerly a domestic servant and at the time of the case a dressmaker in Limerick, sued Richard Copley, an RIC constable from Kilfinane. The couple had courted for over ten years and Copley used the promise of marriage to access money from Mulvihille. Her barrister claimed she worked hard and devoted all her time and energy to saving as much money as possible for the marriage, and she had managed to save between £50 and £60 by January 1884. He kept promising to marry her and at the same time asked her for money to defray the costs involved, £16 on one occasion and later taking another £10 from her. He had an income of £70 a year and had married a woman who had £30 fortune. The jury awarded the plaintiff £40 plus costs, close to the salary earned by Copley. In this case Copley had found an innocent young woman who, on the promise of marriage, was willing to hand over her savings as an investment in her future.[58]

Mary Brien was 38 and her suitor, Patrick McDonnell was 60, when he proposed marriage. McDonnell knew her brother and had asked if he knew a suitable country girl for a wife. On the following day the brother brought his sister to a public house in Tullamore, where the plaintiff lived. The couple met and after a bit he proposed, and 'after the usual hesitation and blushing' he was accepted. He renewed the proposal later, but subsequently married someone else. The defence argued that 'it was a matter of business, not love ... That was what they were, when wanting a wife, to send out and propose to her in the same manner as they would buy a bay horse ... Did the jury ever hear such a story as that of the negotiations between the brother of the plaintiff and the defendant? Where was the first meeting? In a public house. Was it to be endured that a meeting in a public house between a woman turned 40 and a man over 70 was to be called a proposal of marriage, when there was no time to talk of anything but eating and drinking?' That the defence had exaggerated the ages was a common enough ploy in these cases. In the way in which the couple met the defence argued there could be no affection between them. Thus it was argued, this 'contract was an insult and a mockery of a solemn ceremony, and the action was one of that nature that should be discouraged by the jury'.[59] The jury, perhaps understanding the ways in which matches were made, sided with the plaintiff and awarded her £150 damages, and full costs.

IN COURT

As noted earlier breach of promise trials were often eagerly anticipated by the public. The case of Blake *v.* Wilkins in 1817 was so eagerly anticipated that every lodging house in Galway, 'even the humblest in the town was filled to overflowing'. 'Lodging house keepers', reported the *Freeman's Journal*, 'are making now a rich harvest. Beds a pound a night but then it is not so expensive when you get others to join you. Three of us slept in one bed last night in a double-bedded room, and four in the other bed. It was like the black hole of Calcutta'.[60] Blake was retired from the Royal Navy and had sued the widow Wilkins for breach of promise. She was described as a 'vain old lady of 65, possessed of a fee-simple estate of £800 a year'. The court case was the source of much merriment when the defendant's barrister, the well-known advocate Charles Phillips, ridiculed his own client and in the process also won her the case. She was not appreciative and when Phillips left the court Wilkins attempted to attack him with a horsewhip. In the 1841 Cork case of Campion *v.* Drew, where damages were claimed at £5,000, the 'most intense interest and anxiety were evinced by all parties to hear it'. The case was to begin at 9 a.m. but 'long before that hour the grand jury gallery presented a brilliant array of female beauty and fashion'. There were no seats available by 10 a.m., and many women were left standing.[61] In 1863, at a case that came before the Galway assizes the 'court was densely crowded. Several ladies occupied the bar seats, and his lordship accommodated two with seats on the bench'. The case involved a clergyman and the daughter of a 'gentleman'.[62] One case tried in Limerick in 1869 'had been opened before a densely thronged court, including a vast number of ladies of the city and county'.[63] Throughout the period these cases were a considerable source of public entertainment and would have been the talk of the neighbourhood where the plaintiffs and defendants resided.

Much recent historical work has looked upon the court as a theatrical space where witnesses, barristers and judges perform. Before 1869 neither defendant nor plaintiff could appear on their own behalf and the evidence was thus taken from friends, servants, and often family members. Juries, as previously noted, were overwhelmingly sympathetic to plaintiffs, over 90 per cent of whom were women. In the period between 1865 and 1919, of the 401 cases that came to trial, 331, or over 82 per cent were decided in favour of the plaintiff, and 46, just over 11 per cent, for the defendant. People's stories were shaped by the legal system. If a suit involved a plea for damages, plaintiffs would emphasize their reduced value in the marriage place, how the breach had made them ill, etc. It is not clear if juries worried about women making up these stories, even if this was a defence sometimes used in court. There was some public discussion of the possible abuse of breach of promise cases but this made little impact on the numbers of such cases appearing before the Irish courts. A commentator in the *Irish Times* observed in 1879:

> Except the desire to be married, there is nothing the heart of a woman so yearns after as the opportunity of announcing that she is engaged. Nothing can exceed the attachment of a woman to an eligible suitor when he has a large fortune. There is no limit to the rage of a woman 'scorned', as every breach of promise action shows. Starting with these axioms, we find in them, all the materials for the construction of any, the most sensational, legal drama which the episodes of courtship contribute for the enjoyment of a gaping crowd in a law-court. The

solution of it all is that the next best thing to a wealthy suitor is the possession of the wealthy suitor's money.

In O'Dwyer *v.* Maguire, both from Dublin, the defence argued that the plaintiff was a 'clever woman of the world, who knew the game she had to play, and who had entered into a design to entrap the defendant into an agreement to marry her'. She had knowledge, it was declared, of legal technicalities as she had been involved in settling her father's legal suits for debt.[64] This argument made little impression on the jury. Whether women were making up stories or not the juries decided their verdicts on the range of evidence provided, and the likelihood of the events described actually happening. Knowing the significance of marriage to women's status in society, juries may have accepted the plaintiff's case more readily because marriage was such an important aspect of women's lives and a case of breach of promise was likely to damage future marriage prospects. Even when sexual transgression had taken place the jurors remained sympathetic. Despite Eliza McLoughlin, for instance, being seen on another man's knee kissing him, the jury still awarded her £100 in damages.[65] Mary Ellen Fitzpatrick had been seduced by William Vint, both of Co. Antrim, and she gave birth in December 1872. He then refused to marry her claiming the child was not his. The defence tried to prove the looseness of her character but 'nothing tending to evidence of this was proved except that she allowed herself to be kissed by different young men who had seen her home from dancing parties. It was however deposed that this was one of the Ulster customs among the class to which the parties belonged'. She was awarded £150.[66]

Generally the stories told in the court in relation to breach of promise cases were the same. A promise had been made, and it had been broken. The woman, as plaintiff and it was almost always a woman, suffered loss in some way, to her emotions, her reputation, her livelihood or her ability to marry. The cases were presented as tragedies where women required compensation and the restoration of their good name. Romance, love, presents, tokens and sometimes letters were expected to be part of the story. Friends and family were expected to be witnesses to the courtship, the promise and the breach. Plaintiffs were expected to have suffered physically and emotionally from the breach, and this suffering was to be apparent on their countenance or in their dealings with friends and family. Under the direction of the judge, the jury made the important decisions about who won the case and how much damages and costs were to be paid. Given the numbers of cases that came before the courts it appears that women saw this as an opportunity to rectify a perceived wrong, and perhaps, given the success of plaintiffs in securing damages as a way of securing some monetary reward for being jilted.

Women had to present themselves in particular ways in court. Their looks and dress were commented on. In evidence their status, education, family backgrounds, occupations, morality, and character were discussed. In Cork in 1838 in Rubie *v.* Fitzgerald the defendant's barrister noted that Anne Rubie was not in court. He claimed she was older than she stated and that if she were pretty then her family 'would have dressed her up and paraded her and sat her in the back row with a sad face' to elicit sympathy from the jury.[67] Miss Delany, on the other hand was at the 'interesting age of 19 and in addition to the greatest of all charms – youth – she was a lady of considerable accomplishments and of superior education'.[68] Women's age was often an issue, where defendants might claim a woman as old if beyond 30, a plaintiff's barristers would argue that was young. They described women who had not reached the age of 21 as infants, women in their twenties were described as young girls, or as very young. It was common for barristers to claim that their clients had not wanted to bring a claim to court and had only been persuaded of this action by family and friends. In this period women were expected to display modesty, gentleness, passivity and reticence, though in actually taking a case they were making a statement about their own social value as women in a society that prized marriage.

Barristers performed in the court. They were witty and entertaining. They would try to elicit as much sympathy from the jury as possible. They shaped the coming narrative in their opening statements, often appealing to the jurors' sense of justice. In the 1804 Fitzgerald *v.* Hawkesworth suit the plaintiff's barrister asserted that the case was 'calculated to interest manly sensibility and engage the serious attention and sympathy of every man wishing to maintain the moral and social obligations.' The jury would,

> admeasure the compensation due to wounded feeling and a broken heart … They would find the case before them one in which the duplicity and art of the defendant was commensurate with his professions of affection and that the moment he pretended love, he determined to deceive. They would find hypocrisy and love in the same man; enthusiasm and dissimulation, cunning and candour in the same letters; and in those letters, and under his own hand, they would be able to trace the arts and wiles of the deceitful lover. On the other hand they would see in the plaintiff long constancy, continued affection, and undeviating virtue, up to the present moment. They would behold an affecting picture of patience and long suffering, the lady slow to promise, but having promised, most faithful to the last.[59]

In Caila *v.* McNamara, tried in Dublin in 1820, the plaintiff's barrister proclaimed:

> Gentlemen of the jury, this is an action at which the heart sickens – there is no passion of your nature which will not be called forth, pity,

sympathy, sorrow, for an injured woman – indignation, hatred, and contempt, for her betrayer. But gentlemen, whatever sacrifice it may cost you, you will restrain those feelings, and I look for an exemplary verdict from your sense of justice alone.[70]

The jury in that case awarded the plaintiff £2,000 damages. Some barristers impressed the seriousness of the case on the jury. In an 1893 case the plaintiff's barrister observed that 'frequently in actions of breach of promise people look for allusions to the sentimental and tried-to-be humorous speeches of counsel. But in this case there was nothing of that kind ... it was a case of a most melancholy and painful character' and he continues to relate the story of a young woman ruined by a man who had promised her marriage.[71] Barristers also won over juries by their wit. When the defendant's barrister asked what damages were sought he was told £3,000. Pretending to be shocked, he stated he believed that was a 'clerical error' and damages were to be £30, whereupon the plaintiff's barrister replied 'And I at first supposed it was £30,000'.[72] In Meagher *v.* Cross the plaintiff's barrister played considerably to the jury and the court with grave humour when speaking of the defendant who was an undertaker in Limerick. The defendant's barrister following his lead mocked the range of 'widows and spinsters' in the case noting that 'a widow scented a husband as the camel was said to scent water afar in the desert'.[73] It was the humour and gentle, if not sometimes blatant, mockery of either the plaintiff, defendant or the witnesses that kept the crowds coming to these courts. Barristers quoted Shakespeare, Dickens and other novelists. They referred to the classics. Not only were they revealing their own erudition but also that literary culture shaped their own sentiments with regard to marriage.

Barristers also made it clear in court that women suffered differently from men in breach of promise cases. In Little *v.* Lynch the plaintiff's barrister asserted,

> we all know that woman is made to be won by affection ... If a man be affected, he can go abroad and mix in the pleasures of the world, he can go to plays, balls and public assemblies and forget his grief in the amusements afforded by society; but wound a woman's heart once; take her happy home from her, and you send her an outcast upon the world. Win her heart and betray it, and you send her a bankrupt on society, without a hope except that death may relieve her from the canker, which consumes her heart. She is left to the contempt of her own sex, and rendered an incubus on the happiness of her friends and relatives.[74]

In 1877, Daniel Egan from Roscrea, Co. Tipperary, sued Jean O'Reilly for breach of promise. When he was asked by the defendant's barrister if he had come to court 'to recover damages for blighted affections' he stated 'Not exactly'. He claimed his prospects in life were injured, and that although he was only 30, 'it was not since this courtship commenced I began to look older.' When asked if he had been in love with the girl, he replied 'yes', and he believed she loved him. He stated he was 'very much grieved and disappointed when she did not marry [him]'.[75] This was exactly the narrative that women followed in court and it worked for Egan also when the jury awarded him £250 in damages. As noted earlier a small number of cases were taken by men. In the period before 1864, I have uncovered seven such cases. It seems about twelve cases were taken by men in the period after 1865. While some of these cases were successful, in that hundreds of pounds in damages were awarded, many were also failures. As was the case of Samuel Mullen who sued Mary Johnson in 1891, and was awarded £1 in damages and full costs by the jury.[76]

Love and affection were constant references in these cases. The practical aspects of marriage, including fortunes, settlements and living arrangements were well recognized, but romance was expected to some degree in the courtship stage and was always noted when barristers believed there was little of it present in the couple's relationship. Sometimes the barristers declared what romance might be. In the Dublin case of Abigail Bowers *v.* William Morris the plaintiff was the daughter of a respectable gentleman, and the defendant held property near her father's residence. An intimacy sprung up and he proposed marriage. The marriage settlement was agreed and shortly afterwards Morris stopped answering letters. It was then discovered that he had married someone else. The plaintiff's barrister, trying to persuade the jury that there had been no courtship here, asked 'where were all the romantic walks, the moonlight rambles, light and music and all that sort of thing'.[77]

The letters of plaintiffs and defendants, where they existed were read out in court, much to the amusement of the public. One barrister wondered in his opening statement 'why people took so great an interest in seeing old love letters. He heard, as an explanation, that people are very often fond of finding out that others in the world have been as silly as themselves, with an additional circumstance that they have not been found out'.[78] Letters were a great court attraction. Many of these letters were reprinted verbatim in the newspapers. Some were emotional and affectionate in style. Susan Harris made her feelings plain to Thomas Boyd writing that, 'I wish I could put myself in the envelope, for I never thought so much in my life. Although you are absent you dwell in my heart. I think of you most when the moon shines brightly. I close with fond love. – Yours to death Susan Harris'.[79] In Tibbs *v.* Croker, the defendant was a curate in Rathangan, Co. Kildare. The couple wrote constantly to each other and he called her 'my heart's best love' and 'my darling'. The letters contained a 'great deal of religious sentiment'. He then lost interest in her and sent her a letter telling her he loved someone else. Her letters, it was noted, for some time before the break up 'evidenced a teasing, tormenting disposition, which ultimately weakened and afterwards completely deadened the sentiments of love'.[80] Sometimes letters revealed the real nature of the relationship. In Gorry *v.* Maguire the plaintiff addressed the defendant as 'Dear Mr Maguire', with the barrister noting there was 'not much love in it.' She was questioned about Maguire only visiting on Sundays; and then not when it rained. She said she thought he was marrying her for herself and not the money.[81]

There were 80 to 90 letters in evidence in the case of Sutton *v.* Nolan. She was from Cork and he from Limerick. At the end of one of the letters there were 30 or 40 crosses 'which counsel was informed meant kisses', a comment that brought mirth to the court. In another letter the defendant wrote, 'need I tell you how I love you – how every day strengthens that love? No: it is needless, for it has become part of my being to cherish you in my heart of hearts, and to love you with a love that death can only efface. I remain dearest and loved Anna ever your own faithful and loving, Willie,' and he quoted the poet Thomas Moore in his letters to her. It was reported in the press that 'the reading of defendant's letters, which were all of a very loving character, excited considerable amusement.'[82] A number of defendants sought to destroy letters they had sent or were reluctant to hand them over to the court until forced to do so. In Ferguson *v.* Healy the defendant, who was a cleric in Co. Kilkenny, had asked the court to force the plaintiff, who was from Co. Tipperary, to produce letters which he had sent to support his case. However, the defendant realizing he had little chance of winning the case settled before too much was revealed in court.[83]

Just as women were expected to be feminine and demure in court, men whether as witnesses, defendants or plaintiffs were expected to be masculine and vigorous. In Brennan *v.* Cassidy the barrister for the plaintiff noted that when the defendant suddenly married someone else he had left the 'unfortunate girl he had courted for years to be a laughing stock among her friends and neighbours.' It was, he said, a 'shameless, unmanly, and disgraceful thing for a man to do'.[84] Men left themselves open to ridicule when they took breach of promise cases as did Thomas Butler when he sued Mrs Kealy. She claimed that the plaintiff 'had no property in the world but six children, of which he was anxious she could become the parent'.[85] James Murray had also, according to the defence, committed a 'cruel and unmanly wrong' when he jilted Emma Bickley in 1869.[86]

The testimony given in court is by necessity biased. Where both plaintiff and defendant presented their cases, as they were able to do after 1869, there is a possibility of understanding how the relationship evolved and how it broke down. In the cases referred to above we get some understanding of the behaviour expected, and appropriate to courtship. There is substantial evidence that money, and an amount suitable to the class of the couple, was an important element in marriage arrangements, though the absence of a sufficient dowry for the plaintiff did not exonerate men from the responsibility of breaking an engagement. The narratives of these cases were shaped by the plaintiffs and defendants, by the barristers and the judges, and in turn were filtered to the general public through the newspaper reports. It is likely, though impossible to prove, that these reports, including the verbatim quoting of letters, shaped how Irish men and women conducted their own romances.

4. Damages

Numerous factors appear to have influenced juries in deciding the level of damages to be paid. In a substantial number of cases the defendant admitted that a promise of marriage had been given, but that circumstances whether personal, familial or financial had made the marriage impossible. Jurors took account of how long the couple had been courting, whether a reasonable time had elapsed for the proposed marriage to occur, how the defendant, nearly always male, behaved throughout the courtship, the couple's social compatibility, whether there were witnesses to any promise of marriage. They took note of the ways in which the couple interacted in company. The jury's role was, very often, essentially to decide how serious the breach was by examining the contextual details provided by the lawyers and witnesses, and then assessing the level of damages to be awarded. Factors such as the proximity of the wedding date, and whether the plaintiff had purchased wedding clothes, or arranged a wedding feast, helped to determine the level of damages awarded. The jurors were often themselves parents and no doubt were thinking of their own daughters when cases came before them. Lawyers often spoke to jurors in terms of parental care and this may also have influenced how juries decided and assessed damages. Juries expected to hear tales of the physical deterioration of the jilted woman, and her physical decline in the event of being abandoned by her expected husband. Barristers, as we will see later, knew what stories to construct to elicit the greatest sympathy from the jury for their clients.

Money was a significant feature of breach of promise cases. Whoever lost had to pay not only damages but often the legal costs of the winning party and these were decided on by the jury. In Limerick in general damages were in the region ranging from £3,000 to less than £20, figures in keeping with the overall picture for Ireland. Of the 81 cases for which damages were revealed in the period from 1764 to 1864 the average award for a breach of promise was £209. Individual awards varied between a very precise £3,596 in the 1816 case of McCarthy *v.* Grace to £5 in an 1833 case. In the eleven cases decided in the 1830s the average award was £399, an average distorted by the award of £3,000 in the 1837 case of Head *v.* Purdon. Between 1865 and 1919 the average award in a case was £183. According to the judicial statistics the highest possible award was £5,000, which appears never to have been made, and the lowest awards around £3. The majority of awards were between £5 and £200, with over 209, about 44 per cent of the damages, being within this range. In a few cases the damages awarded were so small that the plaintiff had essentially lost the case. In 1883, for instance, Thomas Halliday Kingsley, a London-based medical assistant approaching, as the report noted, 'middle age' sued Miss Eliza Annie Peile of Dublin for alleged breach of promise and was looking for damages of £2,000.[1] The jury acknowledged that there had been a marriage contract between the couple and that the contract had not been rescinded by mutual agreement, but the plaintiff was allowed only a farthing in damages. Technically Kingsley was in the right but the jury clearly sided with the defendant. At the same time Peile had sued the plaintiff for misrepresenting his situation to her, and the jury awarded her the £100 damages she sought, plus costs. Kingsley was thus considerably out of pocket in this case and the jury's verdict and the award of what was known as 'derisory damages' publicly declared that he had been morally wrong to take the case.[2]

One of the largest awards made in the period was the £3,500 damages and £96 in costs awarded to Mary-Anne McCarthy in a suit against William Grace in 1816. Unusually the case had come before the courts previously and damages had been awarded but this second case was taken in order to increase the award. Mary-Anne McCarthy, who lived in Killarney, was a cousin of Daniel O'Connell and he appears to have acted as her guardian. At the time of this trial Mary-Anne was about 18 years old 'of a most respectable family and connections, of great personal beauty, educated with the greatest care, and distinguished for the delicacy of her manners and purity of her conduct'.[3] The defendant, William Grace, was a 'gentleman of high birth ... of honorable [sic] profession, of unimpeached character, with great advantages of personal appearance, a good fortune in possession, and a still better one in expectancy'.[4] Letters were produced in court to show that there had been a promise of marriage. O'Connell testified that the defendant had acknowledged the promise but that given his financial circumstances had asked to break off the match but O'Connell then suggested that the defendant had lied to him about these circumstances. The judge advised the jury that 'if ever there was a promise of marriage solemnly, deliberately, and repeatedly made, this, in my judgment is that'.[5] It was the jury's work to assess damages. They awarded £3,500 to the plaintiff and £96 costs. In coming to this sum the jury took note of the financial circumstances of the defendant and the emotional damage caused to the plaintiff. Grace had, by 1814, inherited a substantial fortune of more than £18,000 and could thus clearly afford the damages. O'Connell had testified that Mary-Anne's health had gone into serious decline since the breach and her 'spirits had suffered a considerable depression by reason of the defendant's conduct towards her', he noted that he feared she would become consumptive.[6] The breakdown of health, depression, a 'changed person', the 'injury to reputation' were the effects noted by barristers evident in jilted women. Sympathetic juries took such effects seriously and awarded damages accordingly.

Further proof that juries considered the financial circumstances of the defendant can be seen in the case of Forrest *v.* O'Brien, tried in Cork in 1845. Dorothea Forrest was the second daughter of the Revd Thomas Forrest who resided in Mitchelstown. Donogh O'Brien was a captain in the military. She was 17 when the relationship began and O'Brien was nearing 40. Again it was clear to the jury that a breach of promise had occurred but the defence argued that O'Brien broke the agreement because he had not the means to afford a wife. His lawyer, appealing to the paternal instincts of the jury, argued 'if your young daughter became attached, would you not shrink from the idea of placing her in the hands of a person possessing nothing but a captain's pay, utterly incompetent to support a married man and a family in the situation which an officer's rank required'. The original damages sought were £2,000 but the jury awarded Forrest £250 damages, and the foreman added, 'that if there were any proof that the defendant had any property beyond his pay, they would award much larger damages'.[7]

In cases where couples were of lower social classes juries generally awarded damages within the context of the financial circumstances of the defendant. In 1877, for example, Mary Gorman aged 27 and a dressmaker, sued John Phillips, a builder, about 47 years old for breach of promise and damages of £760. The jury awarded her £30.[8] Susan Harris, a dairymaid, sued Thomas Boyd, a coachman, both employed in the same house for breach of promise in 1892. She sought damages of £500. They went out for walks, he proposed in the scullery and she said yes and they kissed and the other servants were told of the engagement. 'Impropriety' took place between them on several occasions and eventually she left her employment. By the time the matter came to court the defendant had acquired two houses and a farm. The substantial award of £55 damages reflected his newly acquired wealth.[9] In 1896 a Dublin policeman, who claimed he had 'plenty of money', was sued for breach of promise by a woman 'of his own rank in life'. They had courted for eight years and she had spent £20 preparing for her marriage. He claimed that she had written him insulting letters but was still willing to marry her if she apologized for them. However, it was too late and the jury, keeping in mind that money had been spent on the wedding, and that he was of 'thrifty habits' awarded the plaintiff £50 in damages.[10] A coach builder sued by a nursery maid in Belfast in 1909 had to pay £100 in damages plus costs having spent two years 'going to and from the post office sending love letters to her'.[11]

To put these damages into some context it is useful to note typical wage and income levels in Ireland over the period. These are general figures and it should be kept in mind that there are regional variations in income levels. Maura Cronin, in her study of labour in Cork city, has shown that in 1839 a general labourer could earn between 10*d.* and 1*s.* per day, by 1900 they could

earn between 2*s*. 6*d*. and 2*s*. and 8*d*. per day.[12] In 1885 agricultural labourers
were earning in the region of 9*s*. to 12*s*. per week. An unskilled labourer
working in Dublin in 1885 might have earned in the region of 15*s*. to 20*s*. per
week. Skilled workers were getting 33*s*. weekly. Domestic servants who 'lived
in' earned £10–£12 a year in Dublin in 1901.[13] In 1904 Charles Cameron
surveyed the earnings and expenses of the poor in Dublin and noted that a
tailor could earn only 10*s*. per week and from that paid rent of 2*s*. 6*d*. which
left 7*s*. 6*d*. to cover food, fuel, clothing, etc.[14] In the 1880s the average salary
for a police constable was £75, while a school teacher had £49 and the perk
of a house to live in. Mona Hearn notes that, in the 1880s, a young middle-
class man hoping to marry on £300 a year and expecting to start a family
would have to budget very carefully. Food would have taken up at least 30 per
cent of that income and about 8 per cent would have gone towards the
payment of servants.[15] By the early 1900s a dispensary doctor would earn about
£200 from dispensary work alone. A shop assistant could earn between £1
10*s*. to £2 per week. Leading barristers could earn up to £5,000 a year but
the average earnings were closer to £800 to £1,000.[16]

Some insight into how juries assessed damages can be seen in a case tried
in Dublin in 1876. The plaintiff, Annie Browne, a school mistress who lived
in Manchester, sued William Prescott, who had a dye business in Dublin, for
breach of promise. The defendant claimed he did not know the plaintiff well
enough to marry her, and had insufficient income to marry and that though
they had been engaged there had never been any impropriety between them.
The jury awarded damages of £300 to the plaintiff and had agreed upon this
sum by allowing for two years' wages at £85 and £30 for the breach of
promise. When it was pointed out that this amounted to £200 the Master
stated he could not alter the foreman's verdict and let the award stand.[17]

An award of £4,000 was made to Miss Kate Graves in her claim against
Jonas Morris in Cork in 1875. Both individuals were from 'distinguished
families' and Morris had £15,000 which he controlled when he came of age
and was set to inherit a property worth a further £8,000 a year from his
grandfather. Graves had previously been engaged to John Arnott, the founder
of Arnott's department store, but that engagement had been broken off. There
was no dispute that a promise of marriage had been made and the judge, in
his summing up, declared that 'there could not be a shadow of a doubt that
this contract had been violated and broken in the most plain and decisive terms
by this gentleman'.[18] He guided the jury to consider 'compensation that should
be given to set the young lady in as advantageous a position as possible before
the eyes of those who had been feasting themselves with the scandal and gossip
which they had been hearing'. The jury made a substantial award, which had
the intention of securing the reputation of the woman involved and being a
large enough award to punish the defendant.

Sometimes defendants appeared in court looking poorer than they actually were in an attempt to have the jury keep damages to a minimum. William McConnell, of Co. Antrim, who was 'understood to be in very comfortable circumstances', caused much merriment in the court because of his 'grotesque appearance'. The reporter commented that McConnell's '"make-up" was supposed to have been put on for the occasion, with a view to excite sympathy on his behalf … His entire costume in the aggregate was not worth more than half a crown, and his general appearance and bearing would have led one to believe that he did not possess sixpence in the world.'[19] Other defendants took more drastic measures to escape paying damages. Bernard Collins of Newry had a judgment of £100 made against him in a breach of promise case in July 1893. Within two weeks of the judgment he had put his land up for sale and was later declared bankrupt. There appears to have been some collusion in the bankruptcy between Collins and his brother, Joseph. The judge threatened Joseph Collins with jail if he did not answer questions asked in court.[20] John Meade of Co. Louth who had damages of £475 awarded against him had declared himself bankrupt and left for America in December 1892. Meade's mother appears to have had control of his farm and the money in the bank.[21] Likewise in the case of Sutton *v.* Nolan, where the defendant was the son of a wealthy Limerick corn merchant. In 1879 the plaintiff had won the case and been awarded £350 in damages. The defendant lost an appeal to reduce the level of damages. In 1890 Sutton was in court again looking for the damages, which had never been paid. By this time Nolan was running a business in Limerick but he held it in such a way with his family that it appeared he had no assets and received £100 a year 'pocket money' from his mother, who nominally held his business and with whom he lived. The statute of limitations on the payment of damages was 12 years and Nolan was set to inherit from his father three days after that limit had been reached. The judge suggested that Nolan pay £2 a month to the plaintiff.[22]

In some cases defendants could not afford the damages or refused to pay them. Eliza Hanlon, for instance had won £50 plus £34 8s. 10d. costs in her suit against James Kelly, but he had not paid. He had allegedly sent her a letter with two farthings in it, saying that was all she would get. He later offered £20 in full satisfaction of the debt but the court decided that the full amount was to be paid in installments.[23] Sometimes damages were irrecoverable. John Johnson was taken to court by Hamilton Perry in 1838, to enforce payment of damages in a breach of promise of marriage case. Johnson had been declared insolvent and admitted that the jury in the case had awarded £70 against him, though they also announced him a 'pauper'. Perry was willing to let this judgment go if Johnson would marry his daughter, but Johnson stated he would prefer to go to prison. It was claimed that Johnson's father was a 'farmer in comfortable circumstances'. However, in reality, it seems that Johnson and

Perry were of the 'humble sort'. Perry was advised to withdraw his petition otherwise Johnson would go to prison for a 'very long period'. And the petition was thus withdrawn.[24] In the case of Devereux *v.* Henry the plaintiff was a widow in her forties with nine children, while the defendant was a widower, in his sixties, with two children. The defendant did not appear in court nor did he engage any lawyers and it appears he had left the country. It was evident that he was in debt and the jury awarded the plaintiff £35 plus 6*d.* costs.[25] It is unlikely that any of that money was recovered and the plaintiff may very well have had to pay her own costs. The low award might reflect the jury's belief that a woman of this age and with such a large family should have known better than to proceed with the case, or it might reflect the fact that it was unlikely the damages would ever be paid.

A number of cases were settled out of court, or very soon after the court proceedings began. In 1878 the Limerick case of Fitzgerald *v.* Gubbins damages of £25,000 were claimed. This was an extraordinary sum of money and the highest claim made in the period. The plaintiff and defendant occupied 'high social positions' and both were wealthy. Gubbins clearly believed that a jury was likely to award very high damages and preempted this by agreeing to pay the plaintiff £2,500 plus her costs before the case came to court. The money, it was stated, would be a 'sufficient vindication in the eyes of everyone of the position of the young lady', and would show that Gubbins 'attached no blame to her for breaking off the engagement'.[26] Sometimes cases were settled within the court before evidence was given. This is what happened in the case of O'Neill *v.* Leonard, heard in Limerick in 1902, when the lawyers settled for the plaintiff with £140 plus costs.[27]

COSTS

It is not always clear that the jury awarded costs in all cases, as well as damages. From the cases studied costs in the region of 6*d.* appear to have been commonly made by juries. Even in cases where substantial damages are awarded we still find costs of 6*d.* being allowed to the plaintiffs. In about half the cases studied juries did allow full costs. It is not yet clear, where full costs were not awarded, what percentage of the damages won went to barristers and solicitors. In only a few cases where costs are included are actual figures provided. For instance, in Grace *v.* McCarthy in 1816 the jury allowed £3,500 damages and £96 costs to the defendant, Mary Anne McCarthy.[28] In 1877, Eliza Hanlon had won £50 plus £34 8*s.* 10*d.* costs in her suit against James Kelly.[29] In this instance costs would have amount to about 67 per cent of the damages if they had not been separately awarded. If this was typical then the real value of damages would have been significantly diminished. In a seduction case taken in Co. Derry the action was settled at £100 damages with £75 costs, and an undertaking not to bring a suit for breach of promise.[30] That lawyers and barristers costs were significant is illustrated in the case Mortell *v.* O'Brien. Initially damages of £500 were claimed but the couple had come to an out of court settlement of £60. The lawyers were unhappy as they wanted their costs, so the judge directed the jury to give £60 plus costs, which they did. This suggests that the lone £60 was insufficient to cover the costs of both legal teams.[31] In another case which covered both seduction and breach of promise the defendant agreed to settle and paid the plaintiff £30 for the breach of promise and £10 costs, and the same amounts for seduction.[32] In 1893 the jury awarded £48 to the plaintiff in the case of Meehan *v.* McSweeny. After the verdict, but before the costs had been taxed, the plaintiff and defendant got married. The plaintiff then wrote to the solicitors instructing them not to take proceedings against the defendant though she did not pay them their costs which were taxed at £50 10s. The solicitors claimed that the marriage had been entered into to 'defeat their claim for costs' but the couple's barrister insisted it was a proper marriage and under the circumstances the solicitors had no remedy.[33] In the Trousdale *v.* Stewart case damages of £500 was awarded. The defendant had lodged that amount in court and £200 of this was 'impounded to answer the costs of Mr. Arthur, as between attorney and client'.[34] In a Limerick case from 1883, O'Halloran *v.* Ryan, the plaintiff had been awarded £250. O'Halloran was later declared bankrupt and went to court to have her solicitor give an account of the monies she had paid to him. She claimed that she had given him £117 15s. 1d., approximately 47 per cent of the damages awarded, to cover the costs of the breach of promise case.[35] From the cases cited here costs seem to have ranged between 40 and 70 per cent of the damages awarded.

MORALITY

Juries frowned on cross-class romances, and tended to punish the defendant financially. This may reflect Irish society's general attitude to such alliances. Samuel Clark analyzing marriage patterns in Co. Roscommon between 1864 and 1880 observed that farm families were the least likely to form alliances with those above or below them on the social scale.[36] It was often in these cross-class alliances that evidence of sexual intimacy was revealed in the court. However, it seems clear that it was not the 'immorality' that was being punished, but the sexual exploitation of the woman involved and the cross-class alliance. Unmarried mothers had, by the 1850s, been noted, and maligned, in official documentation by their presence in the workhouse system. Immorality and single motherhood appear to have become issues of public concern in Ireland towards the end of the 19th century when philanthropists turned their attention to rescuing and caring for girls and women who had given birth outside marriage.[37] This attention was focused more on girls and women in the larger towns and cities of the country and we still have no sustained study of how unmarried mothers were viewed in rural Ireland at this time. The moral condemnation of unmarried motherhood became stronger from the 1890s and was part of the fabric of sexual morality by the 1920s.

In a case from 1877 the daughter of a farm labourer sued a gentleman named Boyan for breach of promise. The girl's father worked for the defendant on a farm near Kanturk. The woman alleged she had been seduced under promise of marriage and that the intimacy continued for quite a while. She also alleged that a marriage would have taken place but that the parish priest interfered and endeavoured to get the plaintiff and her mother out of the parish 'under threat that if they did not leave he would make hares and rabbits and worms of the earth of them.' The priest denied making the threats, but admitted to preventing the marriage as an unsuitable one and had tried to get her to leave as 'they were living in sin'. The jury made her a substantial award of £500 acknowledging perhaps the blot placed on her character by the priest, the ability of Boyan to pay and the recognition that he had, in living with her, the benefits of a wife without having to marry her.[38] In a case from 1878, the judge advised the jury to consider that the girl's 'fame, character and future prospects in life depended on their verdict'. Here the defendant claimed he had never made a promise of marriage though the judge, in his summing up, observed that 'if he courted her as he said, the girl must have been very different from most girls if she would associate with him for so long without talking of matrimony'. The judge also admonished the defendant for holding their courting sessions in the cattle byre. The jury awarded the plaintiff a substantial £70 and costs.[39]

In another case from 1895 Mary Dwyer, daughter of a farm labourer sued Samuel Reali, a gentleman farmer. Both were from Co. Tipperary. She was about 23 and had been hired by the defendant as a general servant at £9 for twelve months. He became fond of her, and she noted, 'he said he was cracked about her, kissed her and put his arms around her'. They courted from Christmas 1892 to April 1893. She slept in a loft over the kitchen and when his mother and brother had gone to bed he would slip notes to her through the ceiling saying, 'come down and have a chat'. When her twelve months employment was up, he told her she could stay for another three months. He gave her gifts, and after she returned home, when her contract ended, he visited her there. When she told him she suspected she was pregnant, he told her he would marry her. She gave birth on 27 March. When this was revealed the defence began to argue that this was a case of seduction rather than breach of promise. While the defendant could not deny seduction, he stated he did not promise marriage. He admitted to giving her the gifts and some other clothes. He stated that the farm on which he lived, belonged to his brother. It was 150 acres, and subject to £63 per annum rent. The jury awarded the plaintiff £150, an announcement greeted with applause in the court.[40] Given that Mary's salary, when employed as a servant was around £10 a year, £150 was a considerable sum of money.

Generally in Irish society in the post-Famine period premarital intercourse was seen as the road to ruin for women. Female servants were believed to be most vulnerable to seduction and the result of that seduction was often seen as the beginning of a life of prostitution for these women.[41] It is still unclear how acceptable premarital intercourse was within courtship; that it took place is evident. Women were vulnerable to the real consequences of loss of reputation and premarital pregnancy. That juries in breach of promise cases looked sympathetically on such women is interesting. It may be that there was an understanding that sexual activity within the context of a promise of marriage constituted a different relationship than other kinds of extramarital sexual activity. It may also be true that the vulnerability of female servants was recognized by the jury and no moral judgment was made about their behaviour. The promise of marriage may have been the 'permission' required to engage in premarital sex. This was clearly the case when Eliza Kennedy from Blessington sued Maurice Caddel in 1881. The couple had known each other since childhood and had courted for eight years. After his proposal and her acceptance they began a sexual relationship and she gave birth to a child.[42] Anne Hanna won £500 from John Crosskerry, a farmer of Naggeraknock, Co. Down. The couple had been acquainted for a considerable time and he had made a proposal of marriage in December 1880 after which she claimed he had seduced her. A wedding had been arranged but the defendant did not turn up. The jury awarded her £500 in damages.[43]

In cases where the couple engaged in premarital sex the women claimed it was always within the context of a promise to marry. They also present themselves, or are presented, as passive actors in these instances. They are 'persuaded' or 'induced' into a sexual relationship. This kind of passivity elides any sense of sexual desire that these young women might have had for the men they thought to marry, and this, of course, is in keeping with the general belief that women had little sexual desire. In Gill *v.* Gillgoly, a farmer's daughter brought an action against a neighbouring farmer whom she claimed induced her to 'leave her father's house and go to live with him under a promise of marriage which he subsequently repudiated'. The jury awarded her £70 in damages.[44] Mrs. Ellen Curtin sued James Turner for alleged breach of promise and seduction of her daughter and sought damages of £500. It was alleged that the defendant had paid attention to the girl for some years 'week after week, month after month' and then asked her to marry him. In May 1892 'he induced her to have improper relations with him near her father's house'. A sexual relationship continued and the girl found herself pregnant. A child was born in February 1893 but died in April. Her mother had a solicitor write to the defendant stating that he would get £200, as a fortune, 'if he did justice to the girl by marrying her'. He refused and his barrister implied, hoping to cast aspersions on her character, that she had been intimate with a servant boy in her household, who had since gone to America. The jury sided with the plaintiff and awarded her £150 damages.[45]

In 1877 Catherine Carroll sued John Dalton for damages of £500. The defendant was a farmer living in Co. Limerick and in 1875 Carroll had his child. Her father took a case for seduction against him at that stage and won damages of £40 plus costs. Seduction cases were different to breach of promise cases, though sometimes linked when a seduction took place with a promise of marriage. Seduction, often claimed when a woman became pregnant or had given birth outside marriage, clearly implied that sexual intercourse had taken place and thus a woman was open to a ruined reputation. Seduction cases were tried separately and it was the woman's father or mother who sued, for her loss of service, rather than the woman herself. Pregnancy meant that the woman could not contribute to the household as might have been expected of a daughter. In this second case Carroll was suing Dalton for breach of promise. She was described as 'a respectable looking woman of 30 years of age'. She claimed that he had given her an engagement ring. However, her case was undoubtedly harmed by the fact that she had since given birth to a second child by a different man. Despite this evidence the jury still awarded her £10 in damages.[46] What is interesting about this case is the fact that it was taken at all. The plaintiff had already succeeded in getting damages for seduction from this man, this may have enticed her to seek further damages in a breach of promise case. She clearly felt that her class, and even her immorality as it would have been judged at the time, were no hindrance to her case being taken seriously by the court. In another seduction case the plaintiff's barrister argued that the case should really have been tried as a breach of promise case. In this instance the jury awarded the plaintiff £150 in damages and recommended that the defendant should still marry the girl.[47]

It is quite likely that some women, or at least their families, took a seduction case when perhaps a breach of promise case might not be successful. Catherine Dunne, 'a good-looking, stylishly dressed country girl', through her father sued Patrick Lalor for seduction in 1884. Lalor held a farm of 30 acres as did Dunne's father. She alleged that she had known the defendant for a considerable time, they lived in the same neighbourhood, and he had been paying her attention and asked her to marry him. He asked her to keep their engagement secret and that he would marry her when his parents, recently deceased, had been dead for a year. After this she met him a number of times and an exact date, 26 May, was given for the seduction, which took place in a field near her mother's house. After this she met him and the 'same thing occurred, and was repeated afterwards on other occasions'. She then found herself pregnant and he assured her they would marry. When she told her mother of the pregnancy, her mother demanded he marry her, which he refused to do. Since there were no witnesses, and no letters to corroborate the breach of promise claim success was more likely in a seduction case. The defendant's case was not helped by the fact that he did not attend the court, claiming to be ill and asked that the case be adjourned. The judge deemed him to be 'scheming'. His lawyers could therefore offer no defence and attempted to persuade the jury to limit the award of damages. However, the plaintiff was awarded a substantial sum of £100.[48]

In another seduction case, the girl was 16 and the defendant over 40 when their relationship started. The girl claimed that marriage had been promised and when the defendant heard the girl was pregnant he gave her £30 to go to America to her sister. When the case was discussed with a motion to have it heard in Co. Kildare, where both plaintiff and defendant resided, the court decided that sufficient money had been paid to the girl and the motion was refused.[49]

A point constantly noted in these breach of promise cases was the damage that might be done to a woman's reputation. In 1864 the Revd. S.F. Ferguson sued Georgius Hely for the seduction of his daughter, while his daughter Julia, at the same proceedings, sued the defendant for breach of promise. The damages sought for the seduction were £10,000. The defendant accepted both charges and agreed £1,000 for the seduction and £3,000 for the breach of promise, both with costs. The plaintiffs' barrister made it clear that the actions had not been brought to win money but 'for the vindication as far as possible, of this unhappy lady, and having heard that no want of chastity, no immorality of conduct save with the defendant' and that every imputation of immorality on her part was withdrawn the plaintiffs accepted the settlement.[50] In Case *v.* Dillon the plaintiff, aged 31, worked as a servant for a family in Co. Kildare. The situation was worth £34 a year to her. The defendant, who was nearly 50 years old was expected to inherit a 37-acre farm when his father died. The couple had courted for a few months and a marriage date was set. The plaintiff left her situation to prepare for the marriage. However, the wedding date came and went. The defendant made no defence in court and the plaintiff's barrister claimed that his actions had cost the plaintiff her situation and she had 'in all probability lost her chance of ever being married'. Though seeking £100 in damages the jury, 'given the defendant's circumstances' awarded damages of £60.[51] In McBarron *v.* Dixon the damages sought amounted to £300. Susan McBarron 'in very humble circumstances' had worked as a servant in the

house of the defendant. It was made clear to the court that her 'good name
had not been sacrificed but her peace of mind and prospects in life had been'.
It was also noted that the relationship between the couple had ended in about
1858 but the case was not taken until 1861. It was clear that a promise of
marriage had been made but the barrister for the defence noting the low
circumstances of the plaintiff's family ridiculed the idea that the defendant
would marry this woman. The woman was still in her early twenties, it was
made clear in court that her reputation was intact, meaning that there was no
outward sign in the form of a pregnancy which would confirm sexual
intercourse had taken place, and given her status her prospects were unlikely
to have been harmed by the romance and that she had not pursued the case
immediately were factors that shaped the jury's award of a farthing in
damages.[52]

The moral problems of premarital sex were not a concern for juries. Their
approach appears to have been very practical and based on their understanding
of the expectations women had when a promise of marriage had been made.
In 1870 Ellen Healy, aged about 25, sued Daniel Kennedy, 36, a farmer claiming
£800 in damages. He had known her family for several years, paid her special
attention and courted her, promising her marriage. He then seduced her and
left her. A child was born and died. He offered her £50, which she refused.
Her lawyer pleaded that 'her character was injured; the brand of ignominy was
upon her; she was reduced to something worse than poverty'. The defence
then read some very emotive letters sent to the defendant when she learned
she was pregnant but the effect of these was minimized when it was discovered
that the plaintiff could not write and had a friend construct the letters. This
obvious attempt to force a response from the defendant was a calculated one,
though the jury appears not to have thought the attempt significant. The
defendant denied both the promise of marriage and that he had seduced her.
The jury awarded her £200.[53] In the Little *v.* Lynch case of 1831 damages
were laid at £500. The plaintiff's lawyers noted that the young lady desired
only 'retribution for an injury which, accompanied as it is with insult, has
destroyed her happiness and peace of mind, and it is likely to destroy her life.'
She won £100.[54]

Juries took account of the morality of the plaintiffs in these cases but this,
while it might have reduced the level of damages awarded, did not negate the
payment of damages. In 1856 Mary Egan sued Michael Walshe for damages of
£300. The couple were, in fact, second cousins and the defendant had at one
stage told the girl's father, falsely, that they had married. She followed him to
Liverpool and then to America and a child was born on the boat to America.
There they lived as man and wife and then she returned to her home. Walshe
also returned and married a Mary Neale from whom he received a £270
fortune. The barrister for the plaintiff implored the jury to award substantial

damages because of the 'cruel seduction and disgrace inflicted on the plaintiff, and her heartless abandonment by the defendant'. The defendant's barrister argued that Walshe was a struggling farmer and that Egan 'ought not be rewarded for her folly'. The jury assessed damages at £200 and costs at 6d.[55] In this sense Walshe profited little by his marriage. In 1863, Mary Kelly sued Valentine Fitzpatrick and sought damages of £1,000. She was the daughter of a poor man, but had an 'unblemished character'. The couple lived together for a number of years, moving from house to house and she was introduced to everyone as his wife. Under his father's will he was not to inherit until five year's had elapsed after his father's death, and this date was reached in 1857. He was then worth £2,800 a year with charges of £1,600. The defence noted that Kelly could hardly be called virtuous if she lived as his concubine. The jury however, clearly understood this to have been a relationship where marriage might be expected. The couple lived together as man and wife and the woman's reputation was still 'virtuous'. The jury awarded her £500 damages.[56] Eliza McLoughlin, the 21-year-old daughter of a widow who kept a pub in Lurganboy, Co. Leitrim sued James Harte, the son of a farmer. She claimed that when she was 17, he promised to marry her and they were engaged from 1872 to 1876. In December of that year he married a woman with a £200 fortune. In his defence he claimed that McLoughlin was constantly flirting with men in her mother's public house and it was argued that her conduct absolved the defendant from any promise made. While a witness stated that he had seen the plaintiff sitting on another man's knee and kissing him the judge said that there was no proof that the contract had been rescinded. The jury awarded £100 in damages.[57] In 1872 Ellen Coulson sued James O'Connell and sought damages of £2,000. The defendant was a hotel keeper in Templemore and had business interests in Leitrim. The plaintiff, after leaving school in 1861, got a job in a Dublin hotel, apparently as a barmaid, and while there she got involved with a young man, who had no means, named Du Bedat, 'and the intimacy ripened into something like a love affair'. They got engaged but his family disapproved of the proposed marriage and he left her. She then sued Du Bedat for breach of promise and during the trial she went to stay with O'Connell's family where a relationship developed between her and O'Connell. She kept nothing from O'Connell, telling him about Du Bedat and her hotel work, but he said it did not matter. O'Connell then stopped visiting and she later found out there were rumours circulating about her behaviour, and the defence described her as a person whose job it was to 'lure young men to buy wine'. O'Connell had a barmaid in his hotel and was asked by the plaintiff's barrister 'do you think because a person is a barmaid she is to be badly treated?' He could only answer no. He also admitted that he had kissed Coulson 'very often'. Despite strong evidence that Coulson did not have the purest character the jury awarded her £250 damages.[58] Where

a man and woman lived together as man and wife, or where a clear promise
of marriage had been made, juries appear to have been sympathetic to the
plaintiff. It was difficult for the defence to impugn the character of a woman
where a relationship had been ongoing for a number of years, and indeed juries
and judges disliked defence barristers attacking a woman's character without
solid evidence.

Even in cases where 'immorality' was clearly evident juries could be
sympathetic to a plaintiff. Mrs McElwee, a widow, sued Thomas Hughes and
claimed £1,000 in damages. The pair lived in Mullingar where the widow
worked as a telegraphist in Mullingar railway station. Hughes worked with 'a
wool and butter merchant' in the town. He had first met McElwee in 1890
and within two months of their meeting 'immoral relations existed between
them'. He sent her whiskey, tea and bacon at different times but never
promised to marry her. After 18 months together she asked him if they would
marry and he made it clear this was not his intention and was ready to sever
the relationship if she believed marriage would be its outcome. She relented
as she wanted to keep his company. The defendant declared in court that he
considered her his mistress and that he 'went about with her as a lover and
courted her', but had never any intention of marrying her. It was claimed that
she was often drunk and had been taken home from the 'public house …
under the influence of drink'. The defendant's lawyer, hoping no doubt to
influence the jury in the damages it might award, described the case as 'reeking
with whisky and immorality'. Despite the acknowledged sexual relationship
that existed the jury awarded the plaintiff £300.[59] This woman clearly enjoyed
the company of her male companion and in taking a breach of promise case,
which made her private situation public knowledge, was neither concerned
with losing her job nor her reputation. The expectation of marriage gave
respectability to premarital sexuality. For many Irish women the exchange of
sexual favours may have been a strategy used to copperfasten the promise of
marriage and suggests that reputation was not necessarily harmed by engaging
in such activity. These women were not violating the rules of feminine sexual
behaviour because there was a specific context in which sex was offered. It
was something that appears to have been understood by juries.

Other minor factors also influenced the jury in assessing damages. Juries
appear to have been sympathetic to younger women who sued older men for
breach of promise. In one case from Ballymena the 22-year-old daughter of a
labourer sought £300 damages from the 70-year-old defendant who rented a
small farm. The plaintiff noted that it was only after much solicitation that she
and her father agreed to the marriage and only on the condition that she got
the money and that the defendant's property was signed over to her. This was
a marriage clearly motivated by the prospect of financial gain on the part of
the plaintiff and yet the jury found for the plaintiff and allowed her damages

of £50 plus costs.[60] In a case from 1830, Kavanagh *v.* Magarry, the plaintiff was the daughter of a respectable publican, residing in Merrion and sought damages of £1,000. She was 23 while the defendant was almost 60. According to the barrister for the plaintiff the 'promise was fully proved'. The defence attempting to cast doubt on her character stated she was a barmaid, 'the Hebe of the tip-room, who administered to the consolation of certain good fellows, who met every evening in Patrick Street, at her father's house, against a sexagenarian, who belonged to that class of worthy persons, who in the spirit of thrifty benevolence, write "money to be lent" over their doors.' He had, it was said, £1,400 a year and £14,000 in the bank. In an attempt to reduce the damages the barrister asked, 'What injury has she suffered? ... Surely not one of you will think that she was in love? She might have protested it to the old pawnbroker, but it required a credulous senility to believe her.' The jury awarded £700 though the damages were considered excessive by those in court.[61]

In the case of Williams *v.* Good, heard at Cork County Crown Court in 1876, the requested damages were £3,000. Sophia Williams was 23 years old, while the defendant, William Baker Good was 70. Williams, who came from Macroom lived with her brother and his wife who was a relation of the defendant. Good had lived in India where he had a business and made a large fortune. He was a widower, without children, who returned to Ireland in 1875. Good proposed three times and was finally accepted. In her testimony Sophia stated that she referred the third proposal to her brother and that 'It was ultimately arranged that I should accept him'. When asked by his lawyer if she liked him at first, she stated, 'I never told him that', which gave rise to laughter in the court. The defence lawyer asked, 'If your brothers had not agreed the match you would not have consented? No.' In this case, with the defendant agreeing to a verdict for damages and using the age gap as mitigation the jury awarded the substantial sum of £2,000 and costs.[62] The jurors accepted that this was a financial transaction and understood that a man of this age had little physical attraction to a young woman. His attraction was in his social status and his money, perhaps enough to make up for physical deficiencies.

Juries had little sympathy for men who married someone else immediately after breaking an engagement, or without telling the woman that they were courting someone else. In 1894 Bridget Moynihan, who worked as a cook in Dublin, took a case against Thomas Meehan, a farmer in Co. Tipperary. He asked Bridget for £20, which she gave him as part of her fortune. He then met with her in Dublin and told her he had to break the engagement as his father had left him in financial difficulties and he gave her back her £20. He told her he was going to America. She then heard he had not gone to America but had married another woman with whom he got £80. In a feat of true justice the jury awarded the plaintiff £80 in damages.[63]

Juries also took account of the length of courtship when assessing damages. At the Limerick assizes in 1880, Maryanne Griott of Ballymorris, Co. Clare sued Robert Ryan of the same place, to recover £1,000 damages. The couple had courted for 17 years and the plaintiff's lawyer described the case as 'the most heartless breach of faith that was ever submitted to a jury'. At the time the case was taken the plaintiff was 34 years old, and the defendant 39. The defendant, who married someone else, continued to visit her up to the week before his marriage. The priest testified that he knew of the engagement and refused to marry the defendant to a new wife, but he (the defendant) got a letter from the bishop, which made him do so. The priest's testimony secured the case for the plaintiff, the defendant offered no defence other than denying there had been any promise of marriage. The jury awarded her the full £1,000 originally sought, a rare occurrence, and it was reported that there 'was great applause in court, the galleries being filled with ladies'.[64]

Women certainly felt themselves wronged when promises to marry were broken. Taking their cases to court was very rarely about enforcing the promise, indeed many of the men had married other women by the time the case got to court. In only a few instances did the jury, or the barristers, suggest that a marriage might still occur between the couple. Expected gender roles were evident in the stories told in these cases, women were 'induced' to part with their virginity, men undoubtedly were playing a masculine role when seducing these women. What juries were doing, to some extent, was reinforcing the expectation that men be honourable and keep their promises, impressing upon the defendants that masculinity had its duties. It was understood that sexual intercourse outside marriage could be a dangerous threat to respectability, but within the context of a promise of marriage women were shielded from a loss of character. Thus there was no shame in taking their cases to court, to possibly the most public forum for airing personal tales. Indeed, the court offered them a degree of financial protection, and perhaps vindication, by making awards for damages. Juries were, in awarding damages, making pronouncements on acceptable male and female behaviour. Whereas in general society only women were held responsible for the serious consequences of premarital sexual intercourse, these breach of promise cases, and seduction cases, went some way to place some responsibility on men for their actions and to make them pay for their behaviour.

CONCLUSION

There is much that we can tell from the reporting of these cases but many questions remain unanswered. What impact did these reports have on attitudes to courtship, marriage and gender relations in Ireland during this period? Did people learn to construct love letters from reading them in the papers? Did the success of cases taken by women encourage other women to go to court? Did men, in particular, become more cautious in their courtship practices thinking of the possibility of a court case? Women needed a certain strength of character to take these cases to court, where they were often open to ridicule, as were the male defendants, by lawyers. These cases certainly excited public interest and must have been the cause of substantial gossip in the localities in which they occurred. Yet women did not desist from taking these cases. Did the award of damages make them more or less marriageable? Did these awards pay a passage to America where women might find a new life? How were these women perceived in the community once their cases had been successful? We do not yet know the answers to these questions. The action for breach of promise was abolished in England in 1970, and in Ireland it was abolished under the Family Law Act of 1981.

Notes

ABBREVIATIONS

BA	Ballina Advertiser
BI	Ballina Impartial
BN	Belfast Newsletter
CT	Connaught Telegraph
EC	Ennis Chronicle
FJ	Freeman's Journal
IT	Irish Times
EC	Ennis Chronicle
Nation	The Nation
SI	Sunday Independent
WIT	Weekly Irish Times

1. INTRODUCTION

1 *IT*, 18 July 1870.
2 J. Bourke, *Husbandry to housewifery: women, economic change, and housework in Ireland, 1890–1914* (Oxford, 1993), p. 1.
3 J.A. Nolan, *Ourselves alone: women's emigration from Ireland, 1885–1920* (Lexington, KY, 1989), p. 3.
4 T.J. Rawson, *The statistical survey of the county of Kildare* (Dublin, 1807), p. 23.
5 T.W. Freeman, 'Land and people, c.1841' in W.E. Vaughan (ed.), *A new history of Ireland: v, Ireland under the union, 1801–70* (Oxford, 1989), p. 260.
6 C. Ó Gráda, *Ireland: a new economic history 1780–1939* (Oxford, 1994), p. 249. Figures compiled from W.E. Vaughan and A.J. Fitzpatrick, *Irish historical statistics: population 1821–1971* (Dublin, 1978).
8 Alan Shatter, *Family law in the Republic of Ireland* (Dublin, 1977), pp 25–30.
9 That women took the majority of cases in England in this period is attested by Ginger S. Frost, *Promises broken: courtship, class, and gender in Victorian England* (Charlottesville, VA, 1995), and Saskia Lettmaier, *Broken engagements: the action for breach of promise of marriage and the feminine ideal, 1800–1940* (Oxford, 2010).

10 *FJ*, 15 July 1873. There had been two recent breach of promise cases in the area.
11 For the period after 1865 figures have been collated from the judicial and criminal statistics for Ireland, 1866–1920.
12 *Nation*, 14 Aug. 1869.
13 *BN*, 13 Dec. 1873.
14 Frost, *Promises broken*, chapter one.
15 Ibid., chapter 2.
16 *BN*, 29 June 1857.
17 *FJ*, 13 Sept. 1890.
18 *BN*, 1 Dec. 1851.

2. LIMERICK STORIES

1 See, for instance, *FJ*, 17 Nov. 1821, 5 Mar. 1839.
2 *FJ*, 24 Aug. 1810.
3 *IT*, 6 July 1869.
4 *IT*, 27 June 1870.
5 *IT*, 2 July 1873; *BN*, 2 July, 7 Aug. 1873; *FJ*, 2 July, 6, 7 Aug. 1873.
6 *IT*, 11 Aug. 1873.
7 *IT*, 20 Mar. 1876; *BN*, 22, Mar. 1876; *WIT*, 26 Mar. 1876.
8 *IT*, 13 May 1911.
9 *FJ*, 26 Feb. 1896.

3. COURTSHIP

1 Frost, *Promises broken*, p. 58.
2 *IT*, 4 Dec. 1874.
3 *IT*, 2 Feb. 1895.
4 *IT*, 25 June 1881; *FJ*, 25, 27 June 1881.
5 *IT*, 24 Oct. 1865; *BN*, 24 Oct. 1865; *FJ*, 11, 18 Mar., 24 Oct. 1865.
6 *IT*, 12 Dec. 1865; *BN*, 21, 28 Nov., 13, 14 Dec. 1865; *FJ*, 21 Nov., 12 Dec. 1865.
7 *FJ*, 8 Dec. 1857.
8 *BN*, 3 Aug. 1841.
9 *IT*, 4 Dec. 1860; *FJ*, 5 Dec. 1860.
10 *BN*, 30 June, 1 July 1856.
11 *IT*, 8 Mar. 1880; *FJ*, 8 Mar. 1880.
12 *IT*, 26, 27, 28, July, 15 Sept. 1883.
13 *EC*, 27 July 1819.
14 *BN*, 6 Dec. 1860.
15 *IT*, 2 July 1864; *BN*, 22 June, 2 July 1864.
16 *BN*, 19 May 1854.
17 *IT*, 4 Dec. 1860.
18 *BN*, 13 May 1861.
19 *IT*, 15 Feb. 1894.
20 See for instance, *FJ*, 9 Nov. 1893.
21 *IT*, 12 July 1861; *BN*, 13 July 1861.
22 *IT*, 28 Nov. 1863; *BN*, 27, 28 Nov. 1863; *FJ*, 27, 28 Nov. 1863.
23 *IT*, 26 Mar. 1873.
24 *BN*, 16 Mar. 1861.
25 *FJ*, 29 Mar. 1893.
26 *IT*, 2 July 1864; *BN*, 22 June, 2 July 1864.
27 *IT*, 28 Nov. 1863.
28 *IT*, 12 Dec. 1865.
29 *FJ*, 7 Feb. 1872.
30 *Nation*, 22 Mar. 1845.
31 *BN*, 20 June 1837.
32 *IT*, 26 July 1909.
33 *IT*, 23 Feb. 1896.
34 *IT*, 27 July 1892 *FJ*, 27 July 1892.
35 *IT*, 15 July 1873; *BN*, 16 July 1873.
36 *BN*, 18 Dec. 1879.
37 *FJ*, 26 July 1883.
38 Letter from M.J. Brady, Ballytore, to Card. Cullen, 9 Nov. 1875. Dublin Diocesan Archives, Dublin, Cullen Papers, 322/1 File I: Secular Priests, 1875.
39 *IT*, 1 Dec. 1875.
40 Letter from John A. Dunn, Church Street Chapel, Dublin, to Kirby, 27 May 1856. Pontifical Irish College at Rome, digital collections, Letter 2143, Kirby 1858.

http://www.cflr.beniculturali.it/Patrimonio/IstitutiCulturali/CPI/dig_col.htm. (Viewed 4 Apr. 2011).
41 *BN*, 22 July 1857.
42 *IT*, 19 Feb. 1880; *BN*, 3 Feb. 1881.
43 *BN*, 2 Mar. 1861.
44 *BN*, 19 Mar. 1847.
45 In the Quilter case, tried in Tralee in 1876, John Quilter had murdered his uncle who lived with John's mother. The couple had gone through a 'marriage ceremony' in England but returned to live in Kiltoomey where they 'caused much scandal'. The local priest forced them to separate and they lived in different houses. See *FJ*, 4 Mar. 1876.
46 The AHRC-funded project, 'Marriage in Ireland, 1660–1925', will be exploring the issue of fortunes in this period.
47 *BN*, 6 Dec. 1860.
48 *IT*, 4 Dec. 1874.
49 *WIT*, 11 June 1892.
50 *BN*, 6 Feb. 1852.
51 *IT*, 4 Dec. 1860; *FJ*, 5 Dec. 1860.
52 M. Carbery, *The farm by Lough Gur* (Cork, 1973), p. 261.
53 *IT*, 28 Apr. 1906.
54 *FJ*, 8 Apr. 1897.
55 J. Kegan, 'A young Irishman's diary (1836–1847), being extracts from the early journal of John Kegan of Moate' quoted in J.S. Donnelly, *The land and the people of nineteenth-century Cork* (London, 1975), p. 221.
56 *FJ*, 22 Apr. 1892.
57 *IT*, 4 Feb. 1873; *BN*, 4 Feb. 1873; *FJ*, 4 Feb. 1873.
58 *IT*, 24 June 1886.
59 *IT*, 29 Nov. 1862; *BN*, 28, 29 Nov. 1862; *FJ*, 1 Dec. 1862.
60 *FJ*, 19 Apr. 1817.
61 *FJ*, 14 Aug. 1841.
62 *BN*, 16 Mar. 1863.
63 *FJ*, 12 Mar. 1869.
64 *IT*, 18 Dec. 1879; *BN*, 18 Dec. 1879; *FJ*, 19 Dec. 1879.
65 *IT*, 7 Mar. 1877.
66 *IT*, 26 Mar. 1873; *BN*, 26 Mar. 1873.
67 *FJ*, 3 Aug. 1838; *BN*, 7 Aug. 1838.
68 *FJ*, 4 Dec. 1860.
69 *EC*, 24 May 1804.
70 *FJ*, 14 Dec. 1820.
71 *FJ*, 29 Mar. 1893.

72 *BN*, 12 Nov. 1830.

73 *IT*, 13 May 1904.

74 *BN*, 31 Oct. 1831.

75 *IT*, 13 Dec. 1877. He was awarded
£250 damages. FJ, 14 Dec. 1877.

76 *Nation*, 16 May 1891.

77 *FJ*, 13 Mar. 1840.

78 *BN*, 26 Mar. 1873.

79 *IT*, 27 July 1892; FJ, 27 July 1892.

80 *IT*, 28 Feb. 1871; FJ, 28 Feb. 1871.

81 *IT*, 13 Feb. 1905.

82 *IT*, 22 Mar. 1879; FJ, 22 Mar. 1879,
10 June 1890.

83 *FJ*, 1, 27 Feb., 5 Mar. 1864.

84 *FJ*, 14 Feb. 1894.

85 *BN*, 10 May 1854.

86 *IT,* 6 July 1869.

4. DAMAGES

1 *IT*, 13 Jan. 1883.

2 *IT*, 20 Jan. 1883.

3 *Trial of William Grace, Esq., Captain in
the Queen's Co. Regt. Of Militia for a
breach of promise of marriage to Miss
Mary-Anne McCarthy of Killarney before
Mr. Justice Mayne and a special jury at
Tralee assizes March 27, 1816* (Cork,
1816), p. 4.

4 Ibid.

5 Ibid., p. 28.

6 Ibid., pp 19–20.

7 *Nation*, 22 Mar. 1845.

8 *IT*, 24 Nov. 1877.

9 *IT*, 27 July1892; *FJ*, 27 July 1892.

10 *FJ*, 16 May 1896.

11 *SI*, 9 May 1909.

12 M. Cronin, *Country, class or craft? The
politicization of the skilled artisan in
nineteenth-century Cork* (Cork, 1994),
pp 28–9.

13 H.D. Gribbon, 'Economic and social
history, 1850–1921' in W.E. Vaughan
(ed.), *A new history of Ireland: vi, Ireland
under the union II: 1870–1921* (Oxford,
1996), pp 320–4.

14 Sir Charles A. Cameron, *How the poor
live* (Dublin, 1904), pp 6–7.

15 M. Hearn, 'How Victorian families
lived' in M. Daly, M. Hearn and H.
Pearson (eds), *Dublin's Victorian houses*
(Dublin, 1998), pp 66–70.

16 R. Barry O'Brien, *Dublin Castle and the
Irish people* (London, 1909), p. 387.

17 *FJ*, 29 Mar. 1876.

18 *FJ*, 28 July 1875; see also *FJ*, 27 July
1875.

19 *BN*, 16 Mar. 1861.

20 *FJ*, 13 Jan. 1894.

21 *FJ*, 10 May 1893.

22 *IT,* 22, 26 Apr. 1879; 10 June 1890; *FJ*,
22 Mar. 1879, 10 June 1890.

23 *IT*, 7 Feb. 1877.

24 *FJ*, 7 May 1838.

25 *BN*, 29 June 1857.

26 *WIT*, 13 July 1878.

27 *WIT*, 26 May 1902.

28 *Trial of William Grace*, p. 28.

29 *IT*, 7 Feb. 1877.

30 *BN*, 24 July 1899.

31 *IT*, 11 July 1882.

32 *IT,* 20 Dec. 1890.

33 *FJ*, 23 June 1893.

34 *BN*, 4 July 1860. See also, *BN*, 21 Dec.
1859, 16, 20 Jan. 1860.

35 *WIT*, 14 June 1884.

36 S. Clark, *Social origins of the Irish land war*
(Princeton, 1979), p. 118.

37 M. Luddy, 'Unmarried mothers in
Ireland, 1880–1973', *Women's History
Review*, 20:1 (Feb. 2011), 109–26. For
illegitimacy in Ireland see L. Kennedy
and P. Gray, 'Famine, illegitimacy, and
the workhouse in western Ireland:
Kilrush, county Clare' in A. Levene,
T. Nutt and S. Williams (eds), *Illegitimacy
in Britain, 1700–1920* (Basingstoke,
2005), pp 122–40.

38 *IT*, 28 July 1877.

39 *IT*, 27 July 1878.

40 *IT*, 2 Feb. 1895; *BN*, 9, 11, Feb. 1895; *FJ*,
9 Feb. 1895.

41 M. Luddy, *Prostitution and Irish society,
1800–1940* (Cambridge, 2007).

42 *IT*, 10 May 1881.

43 *IT,* 8 Dec. 1881.

44 *FJ*, 7 July 1893.

45 *FJ*, 7 June 1893.

46 *IT*, 8 Dec 1877.

47 *FJ*, 25 Mar. 1878.

48 *FJ*, 14 June 1884. For other seduction
cases see, *FJ*, 11 Apr. 1831; 4 Feb. 1864;
17 July 1875; 4 Dec. 1893; 29 Nov.
1894.

49 *FJ*, 14 Dec. 1896.

50 *FJ*, 27 Feb. 1864.
51 *BN*, 2 Dec. 1863.
52 *BN*, 2 Mar. 1861.
53 *IT*, 22 Mar. 1870. *FJ*, 22 Mar. 1870.
54 *FJ*, 26 Oct. 1831; *BI*, 31 Oct. 1831.
55 *BN*, 4 Dec. 1856.
56 *IT*, 3 Feb. 1863; *BN*, 3 Feb. 1863; *FJ*, 3 Feb., 5 May 1863.
57 *IT*, 7 Mar. 1877.

58 *IT*, 15 Feb. 1872; *BN*, 17 Feb. 1872; *FJ*, 15, 16, 17 Feb. 1872.
59 *FJ*, 6 Dec. 1894.
60 *IT*, 9 May 1879; *FJ*, 9 May 1879.
61 *CJ*, 18 Nov. 1830; *FJ*, 9 Nov. 1830.
62 *FJ*, 7 Aug. 1876.
63 *FJ*, 31 May 1894.
64 *IT*, 8 Mar. 1880; *FJ*, 8 Mar. 1880.